D1329425

The American Utopian Adventure

BIBLE COMMUNISM

VIEW OF THE ONEIDA COMMUNE.

BIBLE COMMUNISM;

A COMPILATION FROM THE

ANNUAL REPORTS

AND OTHER PUBLICATIONS OF THE

ONEIDA ASSOCIATION

AND ITS BRANCHES;

PRESENTING, IN CONNECTION WITH THEIR HISTORY, A SUMMARY
VIEW OF THEIR

RELIGIOUS AND SOCIAL THEORIES.

PORCUPINE PRESS INC.
Philadelphia 1972

Library of Congress Cataloging in Publication Data

Oneida Community.
   Bible communism.

   (The American utopian adventure)
   Reprint of the 1853 ed.
   I. Title.
HX656.05A27 1972   335'.9'74764   76-187475
ISBN 0-87991-015-1

First edition 1853 (Brooklyn, N.Y.: Printed and Published at the Office of the Circular, 1853)

Reprinted 1972 by PORCUPINE PRESS, INC., 1317 Filbert St., Philadelphia, Pa. 19107

Manufactured in the United States of America

A Book for Students of the Higher Law.

BIBLE COMMUNISM;

A COMPILATION FROM THE

ANNUAL REPORTS

AND OTHER PUBLICATIONS OF THE

ONEIDA ASSOCIATION

AND ITS BRANCHES;

PRESENTING, IN CONNECTION WITH THEIR HISTORY, A SUMMARY
VIEW OF THEIR

RELIGIOUS AND SOCIAL THEORIES.

*" The multitude of them that believed were of one heart and of one soul : neither said any of them that
aught of the things which he possessed was his own ; but they had all things common." Acts 4: 32.*

PRINTED AND PUBLISHED AT THE OFFICE OF THE CIRCULAR.
BROOKLYN, N. Y.

1853.

TO

Mary of Nazareth,

THE BLESSED OF ALL GENERATIONS,

WHO SO BEAUTIFULLY YIELDED TO THE WILL OF HEAVEN,

THOUGH

IT CONTRAVENED THE FASHION OF THIS WORLD,

AND,

AT THE HAZARD OF HER GOOD NAME,

AND OF ALL EARTHLY AFFECTIONS AND INTERESTS,

BECAME THE MOTHER OF CHRIST,

AND SO

THE MOTHER OF CHRISTIANITY,

THIS WORK

IS RESPECTFULLY AND LOYALLY DEDICATED.

BIBLE COMMUNISM.

PART I.

MATTERS OF FACT.

[The head-waiters of the Brooklyn Commune and purveyors of *The Circular*, being under a pledge of some two years' standing to issue the Fourth Annual Report of the Oneida Association, which pledge they have not hitherto had time and means to fulfill; and being subject, in their official position, to many calls for the First Report of that Institution, which they cannot answer, (the original edition having been long ago exhausted,) propose in this work to combine the substance of the three past Reports, with such other matter from *The Circular* as will be necessary to make it a summary substitute for all the Annual Reports; and so acquit themselves of further obligation in the premises. For convenience sake, they will take the liberty to connect their materials sometimes by help of the Socratic machinery of questions and answers, or colloquy; and for this purpose, they beg leave to introduce their readers at once to Mr. FREECHURCH, an imaginary spokesman, who, as they proceed, will tell them all that they will need to know about the singular doctrines and practices of the Communists.]

Mr. Freechurch.—Your servant, Mr. Reader.

The Reader.—The same to you; and I hope we are well met for a little friendly conversation. I have heard of the Oneida Association as a body of Communists living in the State of New York. Can you give me information about them?

Mr. F.—I am well acquainted with the society you speak of—being in fact a member myself; and shall be happy to answer your questions, and to assist you as far as possible to a correct knowledge of their views and position.

Reader.—Where is the domain of this Association?

Mr. F.—On the Oneida Creek, in the town of Lenox, Madison Co., N. Y., three miles south of Oneida Depot.

Reader.—What is the number of members?

Mr. F.—About 150 ; of whom one third are men, one third women, and one third children.

Reader.—Do these all live in one house, and eat at one table ?

Mr. F.—You see in the frontispiece of this book, all the buildings occupied as dwellings by the Association. The main building is sixty feet long, thirty-five feet wide, three stories high, with a habitable garret. The basement is divided into three equal rooms, each thirty-five feet long, (the width of the house,) and twenty feet wide. The first, (in front,) is the dining room, where all eat together. The second is the kitchen. The third, (which runs into the offset on which the house is situated,) is the cellar. Over the dining room is a parlor of the same size, for general gatherings.— The rest of the house is divided into sleeping rooms; which, with those in the children's house and out-buildings, accommodate the whole family.

Reader.—How long has the Association been organized ?

Mr. F.—Since 1847. Many of the first members, however, were emigrants from Putney, Vt., where they had been organized in Association several years previously.

Reader.—What are your principles ?

Mr. F.—Our fundamental principle is religion.

Reader.—What denomination do you belong to ?

Mr. F.—To none of the popular denominations. We are sometimes called *Perfectionists.*

Reader.—Who is your leading man ?

Mr. F.—JOHN H. NOYES, a graduate of Dartmouth College, who studied theology under Prof. Stuart of Andover, and Dr. Taylor of New Haven, and in 1834, while a student and licentiate of the Yale Theological Seminary, became a Perfectionist.

Reader.—Do you believe in the Bible ?

Mr. F.—Most heartily, and study it more than all other books. It is in fact our only written creed and constitution.

Reader.—Are your views like those of Wesley ?

Mr. F.—Quite different. We believe in the ' New Covenant,' which enlists soldiers *for life ;* or, in other words, for *perpetual holiness.*

Reader.—Have you any affinity with the Oberlin Perfectionists ?

Mr. F.—Very little : they follow Wesley.

Reader.—What are your most important articles of faith ?

Mr. F.—We believe in the Bible as the text-book of the Spirit of truth ; in Jesus Christ as the eternal Son of God ; in the Apostles and Primitive church, as the exponents of the everlasting gospel. We believe that the Second Advent of Christ took place at the period of the destruction of Jerusalem ; that at that time there was a primary resurrection and judgment in the spiritual world ; that the final kingdom of God then began in the heavens ; that the manifestation of that kingdom in the visible world is now approaching ; that its approach is ushering in the second and final resurrection and judgment ; that a church on earth is now rising to meet the approaching kingdom in the heavens, and to become its duplicate and representative ; that inspiration, or open communication with God and the heavens, involving perfect holiness, is the element of connection between the church on earth and the church in the heavens, and the power by which the kingdom of God is to be established and reign in the world.

Reader.—Is your social scheme any thing like that of Fourier ?

Mr. F.—We have very little acquaintance with Fourier's writings ; but find, from what we have seen of them, that we differ widely from him on the most essential points. He relies on *attraction,* i. e., the love of utilities, economies, luxuries, &c., for the *motive power* of Association. Our motive power is *faith,* i. e., attraction towards Christ, and spiritual life. He begins with industrial organization and physical improvements, expecting that a true religion and the true relation of the sexes will be found out three or four hundred years hence. We begin with religion and reconciliation of the sexes, and expect that industrial reform and physical improvement will follow, and that too within less than three or four hundred years. He thinks that the Pentecost principle—community of goods —is 'the grave of liberty.' We think it is the prime element of heavenly freedom. We expect, however, to learn many things about externals, from Fourier.

Reader.—What are your rules and regulations, provisions for electing officers, &c. ?

Mr. F.—We have no written constitution, and do not expect to have any. The simple plan of our organization is this : We take measures by religious influence, criticism, &c., to produce throughout the entire body of the society, a peaceable, modest, reasonable spirit in all the members; such that they will be quiet and patient, and give God opportunity to lead them; and expect that in that condition, God will raise up men among them who will commend themselves as capable of taking the lead; that officers will be given to the body from God; not made by vote of the people, nor by appointment of some superior department of government, but formed by natural processes, and, as it were, *born* among them; and that they will be known and received as gifts from God. The birth of children is a work of nature—not of art. The best practitioners do not expect to really effect any thing themselves, but only to wait on nature in the process. The child is created and born by processes that are too deep for us, and that are arranged and provided by the all-wise God ; and all human help in the matter is entirely secondary. So in the matter of making officers; all human help cannot make an officer, or bring one to the birth. A real officer—one who is truly leading the church in the way of God—is a child of inspiration, and cannot be made by man. We can all help the birth : those that are above can use their sagacity in detecting the men, and those that are below can recognize and give place to them. And if there is in all concerned a modest and teachable spirit that inquires the will of God—a spirit of coöperation with the will of God —it will hasten the process.

This is the *unwritten* constitution that is growing among us. I said that we have no written constitution ; but we have a faith in God, in reference to officers, that amounts to the same thing. It is a constitution that exists in the nature of things, and which develops itself among us in proportion as we become intelligent to discover the harmonious, inspired working of nature, of truth, and of God.

Reader.—This explains your method of organization, and officership ; but what is the method of government ? What do you rely on for the regulation and discipline of members ?.

Mr. F.—On religious influence, free criticism, and education.

Reader.—Do you find these sufficient to secure good order and progress, without recourse to arbitrary rules ?

Mr F.—Entirely so.

Reader.—What are your means of religious influence ?

Mr. F.—We have meetings every evening, and they are generally devoted to religious conversation and reading ; though business and other topics are not excluded. Then there is a religious meeting on Sunday, open to the public. The Bible is the daily study of men, women, and children.

Reader.—Explain, if you please, what you mean by Free Criticism.

Mr. F.—It is a system of telling each other plainly and kindly our thoughts of each other, on all suitable occasions. We have introduced a fashion of judgment and truth-telling, which gives voice and power to the golden rule—' Whatsoever ye would that men should do unto you, do ye even so to them.' Selfishness and disorder inevitably annoy the circle around them ; and the circle thus annoyed, in our Association, has the liberty and the means of speaking the truth to the offender. All are trained to criticise freely, and to be criticised, without offense. Evil, in character or conduct, is sure to meet with effectual rebuke from individuals, from platoons, and from the whole Association. Sometimes criticism is given by the whole circle in a general meeting : at other times it is given more privately, by committees, or individuals. In some cases, criticism is directed to general character, and in others to specific faults and offenses. It is also exercised in the discovery and commendation of value in character, as well as in the exposure of defects. Generally, criticism is invited by the subject of it, and is regarded as a privilege. It is well understood that the moral health of the Association depends on the freest circulation of this plainness of speech; and all are ambitious to balance accounts in this way as often as possible. Here is the whole secret of government among us. Our government is Democratic, inasmuch as the privilege of criticism is distributed through the whole body, and the power which it gives is accessible to any one who will take pains to attain good judgment. It is Aristocratic, inasmuch as the best critics have the most power. It is Theocratic, inasmuch as the Spirit of Truth alone can give the power of genuine criticism.

Reader.—What are your provisions for education?

Mr. F.—We have daily schools for children in which common learning is taught, in connection with the fear of God and the law of love. But it is understood among us that the whole Association is a school: and all members, old and young, are supplied with books, and addict themselves to various branches of learning as they have opportunity.

Reader.—Do you hold to community of property?

Mr. F.—The ideas of the Association in regard to the ownership and distribution of property, are stated in our First Annual Report as follows:

THEORY OF THE RIGHTS OF PROPERTY.

" We hold—1, That all the systems of property-getting in vogue in the world, are forms of what is vulgarly called the 'grab-game,' i. e., the game in which the prizes are not distributed by any rules of wisdom and justice, but are seized by the strongest and craftiest; and that the laws of the world simply give rules, more or less civilized, for the conduct of this game.

" 2. That the whole system thus defined, is based on the false assumption that the lands and goods of the world, previously to their possession by man, have no owner; and rightfully become the property of any one who first gets possession; which assumption denies the original title of the Creator, excludes him from his right of distribution, and makes the 'grab-game,' in one form or other, inevitable.

"3. That God the Creator has the first and firmest title to all property whatsoever; that he therefore has the right of distribution; that no way of escape from the miseries of the 'grab-game' will ever be found, till *his* title and right of distribution are practically acknowledged; that in the approaching reign of inspiration, he will assert his ownership, be acknowledged and installed as distributor, and thus the reign of covetousness, competition and violence, will come to an end.

"4. That God never so makes over property to man, as to divest himself of his own title; and of course that man can never in reality have absolute and exclusive ownership of lands, goods, or even of himself, or his productions, but only subordinate, joint-ownership with God.

"5. That in the kingdom of God, every loyal citizen is subordinate joint-owner with God of all things. Rev. 21: 7.

"6. That the right of individual possession of the specific goods of the universe, under this general joint-ownership, is determined by the arbitrament of God, through inspiration, direct or indirect.

"7. That there is no other right of property beyond these two, víz., the right of general joint-ownership by unity with God, and the right of possession as determined by inspiration.

"8. That the right of possession, in the case of articles directly consumed in the use, is necessarily equivalent to exclusive ownership; but in all other cases, is only the right of beneficial use, subject to the principle of rotation, and to the distributive rights of God.

"It will be seen from this statement of principles, that the Oneida Association cannot properly be said to stand on any ordinary platform of Communism. Their doctrine is that of community, not merely or chiefly with each other, but with God; and for the security of individual rights they look, not to constitutions or compacts with each other, but to the wisdom and goodness of the Spirit of truth, which is above all. The idea of their system, stated in its simplest form, is, that all believers constitute the family of God; that all valuables, whether persons or things, are family property; and that all the labors of the family are directed, judged and rewarded in the distribution of enjoyments, by the Father.

"Perhaps the best encomium on these principles may be deduced from the fact that the Association, under the influence of them, has lived in entire harmony in relation to property interests for [six] years, and has met with no difficulty in respect to the distribution of possessions and privileges.

"No accounts are kept between the members and the Association, or between the several members; and there is no more occasion for them than there is between man and wife, or than there was between the sev-

eral members of the family which gathered around the apostles on the day
of Pentecost. The Association believes that in the kingdom of heaven
'every man will be rewarded according to his works' with far greater
exactness than is done in the kingdoms of this world; but it does not believe that money is the currency in which rewards are to be distributed
and accounts balanced. Its idea is that love is the appropriate reward of
labor; that in a just spiritual medium, every individual, by the fixed laws
of attraction, will draw around him an amount of love exactly proportioned to his intrinsic value and efficiency, and thus that all accounts will
be punctually and justly balanced without the complicated and cumber-
some machinery of book-keeping.

" As to the *legal* titles of land and other property, no special measures
have been taken to secure the Association from individuals. Those who
owned or purchased lands in their own name at the beginning, have re-
tained their deeds, and no formal transfer of any property brought in by
the members, has been made to the Association. The stock of the company has been consolidated by love, and not by law.

"The terms of admission so far as property is concerned, are stated in
the Register of the Association as follows:

" 'On the admission of any member, all property belonging to him or
her, becomes the property of the Association. A record of the estimated
amount will be kept, and in case of the subsequent withdrawal of the
member, the Association, according to its practice heretofore, will refund
the property or an equivalent amount. This practice, however, stands on
the ground, not of obligation, but of expediency and liberality; and the
time and manner of refunding must be trusted to the discretion of the Association. While a person remains a member, his subsistence and education
in the Association are held to be just equivalents for his labor; and no
accounts are kept between him and the Association, and no claim of wages
accrues to him in case of subsequent withdrawal.' "

Reader.—Do you carry out these principles, and apply them
to social rights, i, e., property in wives and children ?

Mr. F.—Certainly ; read them over again, and see if you
have any objection. We apply these principles, not only to
property and social rights, but to our ownership of ourselves.

Reader.—Do you separate husbands and wives ?

Mr. F.—No ; but we teach them the law of love: ' Thou
shalt love [not merely thy wife and children, but] thy *neighbor* as thyself ;' and when they have got that lesson by heart,
they *separate themselves* far enough to let in their neighbor.

Reader.—Do parents take care of their own children ?

Mr. F.—Yes, if they please. But members, as fast as they become intelligent, come to regard the whole Association as one family, and all children as the children of the family.— Their special relation to their own children, though it is not extirpated or despised, is reduced to subordination to the general family relation. The care of the children, after the period of nursing, is committed to those who have the best talent and most taste for the business, and so the parents are made free for other avocations.

Reader.—What are your regulations about labor ?

Mr. F.—Labor in the Association is free; and we find that 'free labor' is more profitable than 'slave labor.' By this I mean, that labor among us is for the most part redeemed from the base motive of *necessity*, and is placed on higher grounds. The common anxiety about 'getting a living'— that curse of the apostasy—and the overseer system that exacts so many hours of labor, whether there is a spirit for it or not, are totally discarded ; and in their place we depend on a free, inspired appetite. The men and women organize themselves, or are organized by the general managers, into groups, under chiefs, for the various departments of work. These groups are frequently changed, and constant rotation goes on, so that all have variety of occupations, and opportunity to find out what each one is best adapted to. The practice of doing work 'by storm,' or in what is more commonly called 'a bee,' in which the men, women and children engage, has been found very popular and effective. It may be employed in a great variety of operations, especially of out-door business, and always contributes to enliven and animate the most uninteresting details of work. By such volunteering, *en masse*, the clearing up of a wild meadow or swamp, is done, as it were, at a single stroke; and the occasion is always remembered as one of positive entertainment and luxury. In fact, wherever we can introduce this gregarious, chivalric principle, (as is seen in the case of city firemen,) the otherwise most odious demands of labor, become attractive invitations and opportunities for action. Ten acres of corn have thus been cut up and stacked by volunteers of the Community in half a day, and sport made of it. To draw this corn from the field, husk and store it, would be a long and tedious job for one or two ; but the Association can accomplish it at the right time, and at the rate of six acres a day, with much of the enthusiasm and sportive feeling of a game at ball.

To show further the *effectiveness* of employing this principle, and the amount of work done on some occasions, it may be mentioned that at one time when volunteers were called out for husking, 500 bushels of corn (in the ear) were gathered from the field, husked, sorted, and stored the same day. On another day, 400 bushels were secured in the same way. On one evening it was decided to build a line of picket-fence in a certain place, a distance of 37 rods, and to muster volunteers for the service. In the course of the following day, the posts were drawn from the woods, the post-holes dug, most of the rails and pickets sawed at the mill, the fence put up, and half of it painted ; besides making a new road the same distance.

Reader.—What do you do with the lazy ones ?

Mr. F.—This sort of persons cannot live under our system of religious influence, criticism and education. When cases of laziness or other bad behavior occur, the most common way of treating the offender, has been, to dismiss him from his group, and request him to stop work. This brings on a reäction, and cures the evil in the person sooner than any thing else. We have to criticise members for working too much, oftener than for being lazy.—The world has generally predicted of Communism, a state of looseness, unfaithfulness, imbecility, and general anarchy, in its labor relations ; but we have found instead, that the fruits have been faithfulness, efficiency, order, and an organization growing out of *vital relations,* as much above the organization of the old world, as a builder is above the house he builds; or as a company of organized, competent workmen are better than the machinery which they create and superintend.

Reader.—How much land have you ?

Mr. F.—About two hundred and thirty-five acres: mostly very good meadow land.

Reader.—What do you raise ?

Mr. F.—Most of the articles commonly raised by farmers. There are large orchards of various and choice fruit-trees, growing, and our vegetable garden is very productive and profitable. We have received seven premiums the present season for fruits and vegetables, exhibited in the fairs of the N. Y. Horticultural Society and the National Institute. Mr. HENRY THACKER, one of the best scientific gardeners of the State, is at the head of this department, and under his management, it is intended to devote the greater part of the farm, ultimately, to gardening and fruit-growing.

Reader.—Have you any manufactures, or other departments of business?

Mr. F.—At Oneida there is a large, new building, 68 feet long, 50 feet wide, three stories high, situated on a good water-power, and containing a flouring-mill, a saw-mill, and a general mechanics' shop. The flouring-mill makes the best of flour, and is worked to the extent of its capacity, to supply orders from our friends in Vermont, Connecticut, and elsewhere, where the flour is kept for sale. There are also a shoe-shop and blacksmith-shop in active operation, besides which, the Community engage somewhat extensively in the sewing-silk trade, and in the manufacture of rustic furniture and steel traps. The following is an account of the different employments as they stood last winter, with the distribution of men to each:

Grist-mill,	3 men.	Steel Traps,	4 men.
Saw-mill,	2 "	Silk Peddling,	4 "
Rustic Seats,	5 "	Shoe-shop,	2 "
Broom-shop,	5 "	Miscellaneous,	9 "
Teaming,	4 "	Kitchen,	2 "
School,	1 "	Children's Dep't,	1 "

The several trades mentioned have grown up quite naturally

in the Community, and afford a pleasant variety, adapted to the different tastes and faculties of the members. Changes are frequently made, so that persons can go through the whole circle of employments if they choose; and as spring opens, the above arrangement is broken up, several branches are dropped, and many of the men go into gardening and building operations.

Some of the trades mentioned are a little unique in character, as the manufacture of rustic seats and steel traps, the silk business, &c. They were brought in along with the other private attainments of members, and being adopted by the Community, have thus far proved pleasant and successful.— The Community received a silver medal at the New York State Fair, for specimens of their rustic seats. The steel traps are ordered in large quantities by hardware-dealers, to supply the trappers of the Far West—the pioneers of civilization. In the silk business several men are constantly employed in traveling, supplying merchants and others in the villages. This brings them into contact with business men, and affords a good recreation for those who wish to go out. The trips are generally not over a week or two, and by that time the men are glad to hie homewards. The women are principally occupied in household affairs, needle-work, &c., except that in the summer they mingle freely in the out-door labors of the garden and the farm. To relieve them somewhat from the exclusive and unhealthy occupation of sewing, the Association has recently furnished itself with one of Singer's celebrated Sewing Machines, which is found admirably adapted to the economies of Community life.

Reader.—What is the cost of living in the Association?

Mr. F.—The only estimate we have made is recorded in our Second Annual Report; according to which, the expense for board in 1849 was 45 cents per week for each individual, or about $24 per year; and for clothing, $10,50 per year.

Reader.—What are your conditions of membership?

Mr. F.—Any one proposing to join the Association, ought

first to understand and hold by heart our religious and social doctrines; secondly, to count the cost of enlisting for life; thirdly, to get his freedom from any claims of kindred, &c.; and fourthly, to pay all his debts, or at least disclose them, that we may know his situation. Joining us is like marriage; and these are simply the prudent preliminaries of such a decisive act. If the parties are not in sympathy, or are in external circumstances unfavorable to a union, it is better for them to remain friends, than to venture on a closer connexion.

Reader.—Are you receiving members from time to time?

Mr. F.—The Oneida Association is as full as it ought to be, with its present accommodations. But other affiliated Associations are commencing in several parts of the country, where new members might be received.

Reader.—Can any one leave the Association?

Mr. F.—Of course. When any one is discontented, and threatens to leave, we always set the doors wide open. Desertions, however, have been few; and several seceders, after trying the world, have come back.

Reader.—You say that there are other Associations commencing on these principles. Will you inform me more particularly about them?

Mr. F.—There are gatherings of Communists on the Oneida plan, at Brooklyn, N. Y., Newark, N. J., Wallingford, Ct., Putney and Cambridge, Vt. The *Brooklyn Commune*, numbering usually twenty-five persons, including children, has been mainly employed in the publication of *The Circular*—the organ of the movement—first as a weekly, and then as a semi-weekly journal. Two volumes have been issued. In *Newark*, the Community has been established since 1852 in connection with a Machine-shop, whose business is carried on in common, without wages or accounts among the workmen. They number about 15 persons. Their establishment is prepared to execute orders for light machinery, as lathes, copper-plate printing presses, jewelers' tools, &c. Their address is—'WM. R. INSLEE & Co., Newark, N. J.' *Walling-*

2

ford Association, is a gardening and agricultural Community, of 18 members, situated pleasantly on an eminence overlooking the valley of the Quinnipiac river, about a mile from the village of Wallingford, Ct. This Community has been established since the spring of 1851. At *Putney* and *Cambridge* in Vt., there are small Associations established, similar to the foregoing. Both are located eligibly, as to land; the first suitable for Gardening, and the second for Dairy purposes.

Reader.—Is there a property connection between these different Associations?

Mr. F.—They form one general Community—holding a common interest in all things, and are accustomed to interchange their services freely in men and money. Any means in the possession of one is used for the benefit of the whole.

Reader.—What is the general state of health in the Associations? What are your principles in regard to diet, and what system of medicine do you adhere to?

Mr. F.—The health of the Community is generally good; for instance, there has been no death or serious case of sickness among us for more than a year past. . In several instances persons who came to us, in poor health, have since become sound and well. As to diet we have no restrictions against ordinary food, and as to medicine our system would be properly called *Pistipathy* or *Christopathy* : i. e., it is a revival of the old-fashioned Faith-in-Christ Cure. With Faith, Love and Criticism, we find ourselves able to do without doctors and medicine.

Reader.—From your statements thus far, I must infer favorably of the existing success of your institution, but you have only told me one side. I want to know about the troubles and cost of Communism. Furthermore, it is generally understood that you hold peculiar and radical views in respect to marriage and the sexual relations, which are calculated to repel people who value a current reputation in the world. Suppose we take up this branch of the subject.

Mr. F.—With pleasure, Sir. And I am the more ready to

disclose to you frankly our position on the sexual question, as it forms an introduction and basis to the answer of your other question about the costs and sacrifices of Communism. Let us examine, then, in its length and breadth, the position of the Community on this subject. To this end I invite your attention to the systematic exposition which you will find on the following pages; cautioning you simply not to draw from it any hasty inferences concerning the practices of the Association. It is purely a theoretical view that we are now concerned with, and to this you will please confine your attention. It is no more than fair, however, both to you and the Association, that I should forestall any undue alarm that you may be liable to, about the practical workings of our social doctrines; and for this purpose I will cite two successive statements that occur in our past publications, relating to the social experience of the Association. The first is taken from our Second Annual Report, published in 1850 ; and the second from an article in *The Circular,* published in 1852. A report of the present condition of the Association, (in 1853, six years from the commencement at Oneida,) would not essentially differ from these statements :

EXTRACT FROM THE SECOND ANNUAL REPORT, (1850.)

"The condition of the Association is a matter-of-fact witness of the *feasibility of our* SOCIAL THEORY. Amativeness, the lion of the tribe of human passions, is conquered and civilized among us. If it were not, we could not possibly have held together and prospered as we have done, for four years since the beginning of the new order of things among us, and for two years since we commenced the experiment on a larger scale at Oneida. All men of sense will say that amativeness, in a really licentious state of freedom, will inevitably breed bad business habits, social discords and explosions, bad health, and illegitimate propagation. Accordingly, assuming from the character of our principles that we are licentious, the world anticipates these ruinous results, and confidently predicts our speedy dissolution. But these results have not appeared. The foregoing Report shows an opposite state of things. Good business habits, social harmony, good health, and very limited propagation, are the phenomena which the moralists and prophets must consider and account for. The fact that but one child has been born at Oneida, that was begotten in the Association, (and that not illegitimately, or undesignedly,) testifies loudly for the reality of the victory which we have obtained in separating the social from the propagative, in the sexual relation. That fact, and one other—that of our good health—are palpable and unanswerable contra-dictions of the hue and cry in certain quarters against our licentiousness. We give the prognosticators physical facts—statistics—'figures that can-not lie.' The syllogism we present is this:—Licentiousness inevitably leads to disease, and illegitimate propagation; but there is no disease or illegitimate propagation among us; *ergo*, we cannot be licentious. Will the moralists ruminate on this?"—*p*. 20.

EXTRACT FROM THE CIRCULAR, (1852.)

" As our course has not been seditious, neither has it been unchaste; and those who are fond of imputing indecency to us, simply by inference from our free principles, only show that they have no confidence in their own virtue, except as it is secured by law. 'Mormonism,' 'Mahometan-ism,' 'heathenism,' are epithets easily applied by surmisers of corruption; but they are all false as applied to us. A just scrutiny of the household habits of the Oneida Community during any period of its history, would show, not a licentious spirit, but the opposite of licentiousness. It would disclose less careless familiarity of the sexes—less approach to anything-like 'bacchanalian' revelry—vastly less unregulated speech and conduct—than is found in an equal circle of what is called good society in the world. That we have disclaimed the cast-iron rules and modes by which selfishness regulates the relations of the sexes, is true; but with these conditions we affirm, that there was never in that Association, one tenth part the special commerce that exists between an equal number of married persons in ordinary life. This statement can be substantiated by the oath of the Community, as our general modest behavior may be verified by the testi-mony of disinterested persons who have often visited their friends there.

"And if this is not enough, let the proof of our morality be found in the broad fact of the general health of the Association. No death of an adult member has ever occurred at Oneida, and not a doctor has been employed; many who joined us sick have become well; and the special woes of wo-men in connection with children, have been nearly extinguished. The increase of population by birth, in our forty families, for the last four years, has been considerably less than the progeny of Queen Victoria alone. So much for the outcry of 'licentiousness and brutality.' "—*Vol.* I. *p.* 66.

PART II.

SOCIAL THEORY.

[Re-printed from the First Annual Report of the Oneida Association, with additions and improvements.]

PRELIMINARIES.

This Report would not be complete without a frank and full exhibition of the theory of the Association in regard to the relation of the sexes. An argument therefore, on this subject, prepared by J. H. Noyes early in the spring of 1848, and adopted by the Association from the beginning, as a declaration of its principles, will here be presented, after a few introductory remarks.

1. The radical principles developed in this argument, were early deduced from the religious system evolved at New Haven in 1834, were avowed in print by J. H. Noyes in 1837, and were discussed from time to time in the publications of the Putney press during nine years.

2. The complete elaboration of these principles was a progressive work, carried on in connection with the long continued growth and education of the Putney Association.

3. These principles, though avowed (as before stated) in 1837, were not carried into action in any way by any of the members of the Putney Association till 1846.

4. It is not immodest, in the present exigency, to affirm that the leading members of the Putney Association belonged to the most respectable families in Vermont, had been educated in the best schools of New England morality and refinement, and were by the ordinary standards irreproachable in their conduct, so far as sexual matters are concerned, till they deliberately commenced, in 1846, the experiment of a

new state of society, on principles which they had been long
maturing and were prepared to defend before the world.

5. It may also be affirmed without fear of contradiction,
that the main body of those who have joined the Association
at Oneida, are sober, substantial men and women, of good
previous character, and position in society.

6. The principles in question, have never been carried into
full practical embodiment, either at Putney or Oneida, but
have been held by the Association, as the principles of an
ultimate state, toward which society among them is advancing,
slowly and carefully, with all due deference to sentiments and
relations established by the old order of things.

7. The Association abstains from all proselyting, aggressive
operations, publishing its sexual theory (at this time, as heretofore) only in self-defence, and at the command of public
sentiment.

8. The Association, in respect to practical innovations limits itself to its own family circle, not invading society around
it, and no just or even legal complaint of such invasions can
be found at Putney or Oneida.

9. The Association may fairly demand toleration of its theory and experiment of society, on the ground that liberty of
conscience is guarantied by the Constitution of the United
States and of the several states, and on the ground that
Quakers, Shakers, and other religionists, are tolerated in conscientious deviations from the general order of society.

10. The principles to be presented are not more revolutionary and offensive to popular sentiment, than the speculations
of Fourier on the same subject; and are simply parallel in their
scope (not in their nature) with the theory of marriage and
propagation which Robert Dale Owen and Frances Wright
propounded some years ago, in the public halls of New York,
with great eclat. If infidels may think and speak freely on
these 'delicate' subjects, why may not lovers of Christ and
the Bible take the same liberty, and be heard without irrita-
tion ?

11. The ensuing argument professes to be nothing more than an *outline* or *programme* of fundamental principles, and the original intention of the author was to have expanded it largely before publishing it. The proper limits of this Report, however, rather require that it should be condensed. It is especially deficient in the development of the prudential and transitionary principles which govern the Association in practice.

12. The argument cannot be perused with the fullest advantage by any but those who are familiar with the religious theory, of which it is the sequel.

[The compilers also suggest, that the Reader will find in the ensuing article a formidable array of Scripture references, and that he will do well to sit down before it, with Bible in hand, prepared for serious searching. Also the following remarks, from Dr. Edward Beecher's 'Conflict of Ages,' (though applied by him to an entirely different matter,) are recommended as a good preparative for the session :

"If there is, in fact, a malignant spirit, of great and all-pervading power, intent on making a fixed and steady opposition to the progress of the cause of God,—and, if he well knows that there is one truth of relations so manifold, important and sublime, that on it depends, in great measure, the highest and most triumphant energy of the system of Christianity,—then, beyond all doubt, he would exert his utmost power in so misleading the church of God as to fortify them in the strongest possible manner against its belief and reception. He would as early and as far as possible, pervert and disgrace it. He would present it in false and odious combinations, and thus array against it the full power of that most energetic faculty of the human soul, the association of ideas. He would fill the church and the ministry with a prejudgment against it, not founded on argument and yet so profound as to make its falsehood a foregone conlusion, and that to such an extent as entirely to prevent any deep and thorough intellectual effort on the subject. He would, after succeeding in this, paralyze them with an effeminate timidity with reference even to any serious and thorough discussion of the subject ; so that even men who are in general the boldest advocates of free inquiry shall tremble and grow pale at the thought that any one with whom they are associated shall dare to avow an open and firm belief of the proscribed truth."—*Conflict of Ages, p.* 223.]

BIBLE ARGUMENT;
Defining the Relations of the Sexes in the Kingdom of Heaven.

CHAPTER I.

Showing what is properly to be anticipated concerning the coming of the Kingdom of Heaven and its institutions on earth.

PROPOSITION I.—The Bible predicts the coming of the kingdom of heaven on earth. Dan. 2: 44. Isa. 25: 6—9.

Note.—The religious world has constantly professed to be in expectation of the kingdom of heaven, and especially for the last thirty years. The popular hope of the Millennium, the universal use of the Lord's prayer, and the accumulating fervor of the public mind in relation to the Second Advent, Universal Reform, new theories of Society, Spiritual Manifestations, &c. &c., are varied manifestations of that expectation.

PROPOSITION II.—The administration of the will of God in his kingdom on earth, will be the same as the administration of his will in heaven. Matt. 6: 10. Eph. 1: 10.

Note.—If we pray '*Thy will be done on earth, as it is done in heaven,*' we ought not to shrink from filling out that prayer by asking specifically for whatever we know to be according to the will of God as it is done in heaven. For instance, we know that sin, disease and death, are banished from heaven. We ought then to pray that they may be banished from earth; and if we pray for these things, we ought to expect them; and if we expect them, we ought to labor for them; and if we labor for them, we ought to begin by clearing away all doctrines that deny the possibility of them.

PROPOSITION III.—In heaven God reigns over body, soul, and estate, without interference from human governments; and consequently, the advent of his kingdom on earth will supplant all human governments. Dan. 2: 44. 1 Cor. 15: 24, 25. Isa. 26: 13, 14, and 33: 22.

Note.—In the introduction of the kingdom of heaven on earth, the citizens of that kingdom will necessarily be called to positions and duties, different from those of the Primitive church. The object in view at the beginning of the Christian dispensation, was not to establish the kingdom of heaven on earth immediately, but to march an isolated church through the world, establish the kingdom in the heavens, and prepare the way for the kingdom on earth, by giving the Gentiles the Bible and religious training. It was not the business of the Primitive church to supplant the governments of this world. Hence they were directed to submit to the 'powers that be.' But at the end of 'the times of the Gentiles' the church of God will be called to break in pieces 'the powers that be,' and take the place of them. This is necessarily implied in the proof of the third proposition above. (See also Dan. 7: 22, 27.) This difference of positions is a sufficient general answer to those who insist on a literal subjection of the present church to the precepts of the Primitive church concerning civil governments and institutions.

Illustration.—An army sent into a foreign territory for military purposes simply, is placed under the rules of martial discipline, which have reference to hostile surroundings and are very restrictive. Such was the case of the Primitive church. But an army sent for the purpose of introducing civil institutions and settling in a foreign territory, ought to pass, as soon as it can do so safely, from the restrictions of martial law, to the conditions of permanent civilized life. Such is the position of the church which is called to introduce the kingdom of heaven on earth.

PROPOSITION IV.—The institutions of the kingdom of heaven are of such a nature, that the general disclosure of them in the apostolic age would have been inconsistent with the continuance of the institutions of the world through the times of the Gentiles. They were not, therefore, brought out in detail on the surface of the Bible, but were disclosed verbally (more or less) by Paul and others, to the interior part of the church. 1 Cor. 2: 6. 2 Cor. 12: 4. John 16: 12, 13. (Compare John 3: 12.) Heb. 9: 5, in the original. The holy of holies in the temple, which was veiled from all but the High Priest, symbolized heaven. It was necessary that the veil should remain between the world and heaven, till the end of the times of the Gentiles. Then it is to be removed. Rev. 11: 15—19.

Note 1.—Christ charged his disciples not to publish all the truths he had committed to them, in the injunction, 'Cast not your pearls before swine;' and, on the other hand, he forbore to tell *them* many things which were in his heart, because they were 'not able to bear them.' In his conversation with Nicodemus, he signified, that there was a class of interior truths, which he called 'heavenly things,' more incredible and unintelligible to the sensual understanding by far, than the doctrine of regeneration that Nicodemus made so great a mystery of; *that* he classed among earthly things, as a doctrine which every teacher in Israel ought to be familiar with, and said, 'If I have told you earthly things and you believe not, how shall ye believe if I tell you of heavenly things?' He was prepared to reveal heavenly things, but Nicodemus was not prepared to believe even earthly things. He promised his disciples that the Spirit of truth which he would send, should lead them into these interior truths; but they observed his caution and example, and did not cast them before swine, or reveal them prematurely to any who could not bear them, by committing them to writing. Paul refers to heavenly things when he says, 'We speak wisdom among them that are perfect.' The Corinthians to whom he was writing, 'were yet carnal;' he could not speak unto them as unto spiritual; but he stirred up their ambition to become spiritual, that they might know the deep things of God. When he was caught up into paradise, he heard 'unspeakable words' that it was 'not *lawful* for a man to utter.'

Note 2.—From the foregoing it follows, that we cannot reasonably look for a parade of proof-texts, specifically sanctioning every change which the kingdom of heaven is to make in the institutions of the world. It is to be assumed that the church which is called to introduce that kingdom will have the same spiritual understanding which was the key to the unwritten mysteries of the inner sanctuary in Paul's time. It is enough, if the Bible furnishes radical principles on which a spiritual mind can stand and reason firmly concerning things within the veil. The Bible must not be asked to lead us step by step into the holy of holies, but only to point the way, consigning us to the specific guidance of 'the spirit of wisdom and revelation.' Eph. 1: 17.

CHAPTER II.

Showing that Marriage is not an institution of the Kingdom of Heaven, and must give place to Communism.

PROPOSITION v.—In the kingdom of heaven, the institution of marriage which assigns the exclusive possession of one woman to one man, does not exist. Matt. 22: 23—30. 'In the resurrection they neither marry nor are given in marriage.'

Note.—Christ, in the passage referred to, does not exclude the sexual distinction, or sexual intercourse, from the heavenly state, but only the world's method of assigning the sexes to each other, which alone, creates the difficulty presented in the question of the Sadducees. Their question evidently referred only to the matter of *ownership.* Seven men had been married to one woman, and dying successively, the question was, whose she should be in the resurrection. Suppose the question had been asked, in reference to Slavery instead of marriage, thus: A man owning a slave dies and leaves him to his brother; he dying, bequeaths him to the next brother, and so seven of them in succession own this slave; now whose slave shall he be in the resurrection? This, evidently, is the amount of the Sadducees' question, and Christ's answer is as though he had said that in the resurrection there are neither slaves nor slaveholders. It is a nullification of the idea of marriage ownership. Can any thing more be made of it? To assume from this passage a nullification of the sexual relation, as the Shakers and others do, is as absurd as it would be to assume that because there is no slavery, there is therefore no serving one another in the resurrection; whereas the gospel teaches that there is more serving one another there than in the world. The constitutional distinctions and offices of the sexes belong to their original paradisaical state; and there is no proof in the Bible or in reason, that they are ever to be abolished, but abundance of proof to the contrary. 1 Cor. 11: 3—11. The saying of Paul that in Christ 'there is neither Jew nor Greek, *neither male nor female,*' &c., simply means that the unity of life which all the members of Christ have in him, overrides all individual distinctions. In the same sense as that in which the apostle excludes distinction of *sexes,* he also virtually excludes distinction of persons; for he adds, 'Ye are all *one* in Christ Jesus.' Yet the several members of Christ, in perfect consistency with their spiritual unity, remain distinct persons; and so the sexes, though one in their innermost life, as members of Christ, yet retain their constitutional distinctions.

PROPOSITION VI.—In the kingdom of heaven, the intimate union of life and interests, which in the world is limited to pairs, extends through the whole body of believers; i. e. *complex* marriage takes the place of simple. John 17: 21. Christ prayed that *all* believers might be one, *even as* he and the Father are one. His unity with the Father is defined in the words, '*All mine are thine, and all thine are mine.*' Ver. 10. This perfect community of interests, then, will be the condition of *all,* when his prayer is answered. The universal unity of the members of Christ, is described in the same terms that are used to describe marriage-unity. Compare 1 Cor. 12: 12—27, with Gen. 2: 24. See also 1 Cor. 6: 15—17, and Eph. 5: 30—32.

Note.—Love between the children of God, is excited and developed by a motive similar to that which produces ordinary *family affection.*—'Every one that loveth him that begat, loveth also him that is begotten of him.' 1 John 5: 1. The exciting cause is not sexuality, or any other external quality, but the fact that the parties have one Father, and of course, one life. The sons and daughters of God, must have even a stronger sense of their blood-relationship than ordinary brothers and sisters; because the Spirit of the Father, by which they are begotten, is their abiding Comforter, always renewing their consciousness of unity with him and with each other. Marriage, in the world, requires a man to '*leave father and mother and cleave unto his wife.*' But the sons and daughters of God can never leave *their* Father and mother. Of course, the paramount sexual affection, required by the law of marriage, can have no place among them. They live as children with their Father forever, and the paramount affection of the household is not sexual, but *brotherly* love, an affection that grows directly out of the common relationship to the Father, and of course is as universal as that relationship, and as appropriate between male and male, as between male and female. This affection as it exists between the different sexes, is necessarily unlimited as to number. A brother may love ten sisters, or a sister ten brothers, according to the customs of the world. The exclusiveness of marriage does not enter the family circle. But heaven is a family circle; and when we say that brotherly love is the *paramount* affection of that circle, we mean that it takes the place of supremacy which the matrimonial affection occupies in this world; it is that by which the members of God's family are brought into the closest possible union; that which controls and directs the sexual, as well as every other subordinate affection. For this reason there is neither marrying nor giving in marriage in the resurrection. Marriage makes of '*twain one flesh,*' but the brotherly love of heaven, makes of *all one spirit.* The unity of *all* God's family is described in Christ's prayer, John 17: 21—23, as far more complete, than any that earthly imaginations conceive of as existing in the conjugal relation.

PROPOSITION VII.—The effects of the effusion of the Holy Spirit on the day of Pentecost, present a practical commentary on Christ's prayer for the unity of believers, and a sample of the tendency of heavenly influences, which fully confirm the foregoing proposition. 'All that believed were together, and had all things common ; and sold their possessions and goods, and parted them to all, as every man had need.'— 'The multitude of them that believed were of one heart and of one soul ; neither said any of them that aught of the things which he possessed was his own; but they had all things common.' Acts 2: 44, 45, and 4: 32. Here is unity like that of the Father and the Son : 'All mine thine, and all thine mine.'

Note 1.—The unity of the day of Pentecost is not to be regarded as temporary and circumstantial.   On the contrary, the accommodation to the fashion of the world, which succeeded and overlaid it in the apostolic age, was the transitory state of the church, and Pentecostal community of interests was its final and permanent condition in the heavens.   The spirit of heaven manifested its nature and tendency for a moment, and then gave way for a season to the institutions of the world.   The seed of heavenly unity fell into the earth, and was buried for a time, but in the harvest at the Second Coming it was reproduced, and became the universal and eternal principle of the church.

Note 2.—Even under the straitened policy of the times subsequent to the day of Pentecost, we can discover the workings of the principles of Heavenly Association in the management of property.   Many hints occur throughout the New Testament, which prove, that after the first outburst of the Community spirit on the day of Pentecost had been suppressed by persecution, the various churches formed themselves into a great mutual insurance company, as it might be called, which guaranteed their members against poverty.   It is evident, that the whole substance of each was pledged for the support of all.   It was in this way that they realized Christ's promise, that those who forsook all for him, should have 'an hundred-fold in this present life,' of the very things they gave up.   That promise certainly was not, and could not be, fulfilled in any other way.— The Community spirit was carried into practice as far as possible, without coming into collision with surrounding institutions, and far enough to provide sustenance for all during their stay previous to Christ's coming.— Paul was the chief commissioner through whose agency the scattered churches bore one another's burdens ; and distribution was made to every man as every man had need.   He says to the Corinthians, "I mean not that other men be eased and you burdened; but by an equality, that now at this time your abundance may be a supply for their want, that their abundance also may be a supply for your want; that there may be an equality, as it is written: He that had gathered much had nothing over, and he that had gathered little had no lack." 2 Cor. 8: 13—15.   This certainly is in essence actual Communism.

Note 3.—We admit that the community principle of the day of Pentecost, in its actual operation at that time, extended only to goods and chattels.   Yet we affirm that there is no intrinsic difference between property in persons and property in things ; and that the same spirit which abolished exclusiveness in regard to money, would abolish, if circumstances allowed full scope to it, exclusiveness in regard to women and children.— As we infer that a solvent which has corroded the surface of a stone, would consume the whole of it, if allowed a full operation, so we infer from the operation of the spirit of heaven on the day of Pentecost, partial and temporary though it was, that in a continuous and perfect experiment, that spirit would consume all exclusiveness.   The reason why a partial and temporary experiment only was exhibited, may be inferred from what has already been said in relation to the difference of times. (See Note to Prop. iii, and Prop. iv.) The world was not ripe for a thorough revolution even in regard to property, and much less in regard to sexual morality. A momentary operation of the community-spirit on property exclusiveness was tolerated, but the experiment could go no further without a destructive collision with civil government, which was not according to the design of God at that time.

Note 4.—Paul expressly places property in women and property in goods in the same category, and speaks of them together, as ready to be abolished by the advent of the kingdom of heaven. 'The time,' says he, 'is short; it remaineth that they that have wives be as though they had none;....and they that buy as though they possessed not;....for the fashion of this world passeth away.' (1 Cor. 7: 29—31.) On the day of Pentecost, 'they that bought were as though they possessed not.' The fashion of the world passed away in regard to property, for the time being. It is fair to infer from Paul's language, that the fashion of the world in regard to wives was, in his view, to pass away in the same manner ; i. e., that exclusiveness was to be abolished, and free love or complex-marriage take its place, in the heavenly state into which the church was about entering.

PROPOSITION VIII.—The abolishment of appropriation is involved in the very nature of a true relation to Christ in the gospel. This we prove thus :—The *possessive* feeling which expresses itself by the possessive pronoun *mine*, is the same in essence, when it relates to women, as when it relates to money, or any other property. Amativeness and acquisitiveness are only different channels of one stream. They converge as we trace them to their source. Grammar will help us to ascertain their common centre ; for the possessive pronoun *mine*, is derived from the personal pronoun *I;* and so the possessive feeling, whether amative or acquisitive, flows from the personal feeling, i. e., is a branch of *egotism.* Now egotism is abolished by the gospel relation to Christ. The grand mystery of the gospel is vital union with Christ—the merging of self in his life—the extinguishment of the pronoun *I* at the spiritual centre. Thus Paul says, ' I live, *yet not I,* but Christ liveth in me.' The grand distinction between the Christian and the unbeliever—between heaven and the world—is, that

in one reigns the *we-spirit*, and in the other the *I-spirit*.—
From *I* comes *mine*, and from the *I-spirit* comes exclusive
appropriation of money, women, &c. From *we* comes *ours*,
and from the *we-spirit* comes universal community of interests.

PROPOSITION IX.—The abolishment of sexual exclusiveness
is involved in the love-relation required between all believers
by the express injunction of Christ and the apostles, and by
the whole tenor of the New Testament. 'The new commandment is, that we love one another,' and that, not by pairs, as
in the world, but *en masse*. We are required to love one another *fervently*, (1 Peter 1: 22,) or, as the original might be
rendered, *burningly*. The fashion of the world forbids a man
and woman who are otherwise appropriated, to love one another burningly—to flow into each other's hearts. But if they
obey Christ they must do this; and whoever would allow them
to do this, and yet would forbid them (on any other ground
than that of present expediency) to express their unity of
hearts by bodily unity, would 'strain at a gnat and swallow a
camel;' for unity of hearts is as much more important than
the bodily expression of it, as a camel is bigger than a gnat.

Note.—The tendency of religious unity to flow into the channel of amativeness, manifests itself in revivals and in all the higher forms of spiritual-
ism. Marriages or illegitimate amours usully follow religious excitements.
Almost every spiritual sect has been troubled by amative tendencies. These
facts are not to be treated as unaccountable irregularities, but as expressions of a law of human nature. Amativeness is in fact (as will be seen
more fully hereafter) the first and most natural channel of religious love.
This law must not be despised and ignored, but must be investigated and
provided for. This is the object of the present treatise.

PROPOSITION X.—The abolishment of worldly restrictions
on sexual intercourse, is involved in the anti-legality of the
gospel. It is incompatible with the state of perfected freedom towards which Paul's gospel of 'grace without law'
leads, that man should be allowed and required to *love* in all
directions, and yet be forbidden to *express* love in its most
natural and beautiful form, except in one direction. In fact,
Paul says with direct reference to sexual intercourse—'All

things are *lawful* for me, but all things are not expedient;'
all things are lawful for me, but I will not be brought under
the power of any;' (1Cor. 6: 12 ;) thus placing the restrictions which were necessary in the transition period on the
basis, not of law, but of expediency and the demands of
spiritual freedom, and leaving it fairly to be inferred that in
the final state, when hostile surroundings and powers of bondage cease, all restrictions also will cease.

Note.—The philosophy of love and its expression is this : love in all its
forms, is simply *attraction,* or the tendency of congenial elements to approach and become one. The attraction between the magnet and the steel
is a familiar illustration of the nature of love. The most important difference between the two is, that while the attraction of inanimate substances
is wholly involuntary, love, or the attraction of life towards life, is modified
by the will. Volition can concentrate and quicken congenial elements, and
so can increase love ; but it cannot create congeniality, and therefore it can
only modify, not create love. So that the essence of love is attraction,
whether it is modified by the will or not. This, then, we repeat, is the
nature of love in all its forms—as well between God and man, and between
man and man, as between man and woman—as well between the highest
spheres of spiritual life, as between the lowest sensual elements. Life seeks
unity with congenial life, and finds happiness in commingling. Love while
seeking unity, is *desire*—*in* unity, it is *happiness.* The commands of the
Bible to love God and his family, and not to love the world, are commands
to exercise the will in favoring profitable, i. e. spiritual attractions, and in
denying unprofitable, i. e. fleshly attractions.

In a perfect state of things, where corrupting attractions have no place,
and all susceptibilities are duly surbordinated and trained, the denying
exercise of the will ceases, and attraction reigns without limitation. In
such a state, what is the difference between the love of man towards
man, and that of man towards woman ? Attraction being the essence of
love in both cases, the difference lies in this, that man and woman are so
adapted to each other by the differences of their natures, that attraction
can attain a more perfect union between them than between man and man,
or between woman and woman. Attraction between the magnet and the
steel is the same in essence, whatever may be the forms of the surfaces
presented for contact. If a positive obstruction intervenes. the steel
advances to the obstructing substance, and there stops. If nothing intervenes, and the tangent ends are plane surfaces, the steel advances to plane
contact. If the tangent ends are ball and socket, or mortise and tenon, the
steel, seeking by the law of attraction the closest possible unity, advances to
interlocked contact. So love, restrained by law and the will, as in the world,

is stopped by positive obstructions; love between man and man can only advance to something like plain contact; while love between man and woman can advance to interlocked contact. In other words, love between the different sexes, is peculiar, not in its essential nature, but because they are so constructed with reference to each other, both spiritually and physically, (for the body is an index of the life,) that more intimate unity, and of course more intense happiness in love, is possible between them than between persons of the same sex.

Now in a state of unobstructed love, it is as certain that attraction acting between man and woman, will seek its natural expression in sexual intercourse, as that the magnet and steel will approach each other as near as possible, or as that the attraction between man and man will seek its natural expression in the 'kiss of charity' or the embrace; and legal obstructions are no more compatible with spiritual freedom and rational taste in one case than in the other. It was manifestly the design of God in creating the sexes, to give love more intense expression than is possible between persons of the same sex; and it is foolish to imagine that he will ever abandon that design by unsexing his children, or impede it by legal restrictions on sexual intercourse, in the heavenly state.

PROPOSITION XI.—The abolishment of the marriage system is involved in Paul's doctrine of the end of ordinances. Marriage is one of the 'ordinances of the worldly sanctuary.'—This is proved by the fact that it has no place in the resurrection. (See Proposition 5.) The Roman Catholic church places it among its seven *sacraments.* (See Power's Catholic Manual, pp. 29, 185.) Paul expressly limits it to life in the flesh. Rom. 7: 2, 3. The assumption, therefore, that believers are dead to the world by the death of Christ, (which authorized the abolishment of Jewish ordinances,) legitimately makes an end of marriage. Col. 2: 20.

Note 1.—Marriage stands on the same basis with the Sabbath. Both may be *defended,* on the ground of the sanction of the decalogue, and of their necessity and usefulness. Both may be *assailed,* on the ground of their legality and unprofitableness. Both are 'shadows of good things to come.' As one day in seven is to a perpetual Sabbath, so marriage in pairs is to the universal marriage of the church of Christ.

Note 2.—The abolishment of the Jewish ordinances was the 'offense of the cross' in the apostolic age. Gal. 5: 11, & 6: 12. The nullification of circumcision was as revolting and impious to the Jew, as the nullification of marriage can be to the Gentile. Written commandments were as formidably arrayed against the spiritual doctrines of the new church in the one case, as they are in the other. The clash of the moral conscience with the spiritual, was as complete in the one case as it is in the other. God's old orders confronted his new. The apostles had even less warrant in the Old Testament for their attack on the Jewish ritual, than we have in the whole Bible for our attack on marriage. The primitive 'offense of the cross' brought the church into collision with the civil as well as the ecclesiastical authorities, compelled believers to die substantially to the world at the outset, and exposed them to constant persecution and the hazard of literal death. If the spirit of Christ and of the unbelieving world are as hostile to each other now as ever, (which is certainly true,) it is clear that the cross of Christ must have a development in the dispensation of the fullness of times, as offensive to the Gentile world, as its nullification of the Sinai law was to the Jewish world. Where then shall we look for the present 'offense of the cross?' How shall the gospel of death to the world by the death of Christ, protrude itself in a practical form, as it did in the apostolic age, and attack the central life of the Gentile world? The offense cannot come on the same point as it did in the Primitive church; for the special ordinances of Judaism have passed away. The same may be said of the ordinances of Popery, so far as the most important part of the religious world is concerned. The nullification of the ordinances of the popular Protestant sects, cannot be a full 'offense of the cross,' corresponding to the primitive offense; first, because the *ecclesiastical* authority of those sects is feeble, divided, and clashing; and secondly, because they have no *civil* authority; so that emancipation from the ordinances of any one of them is only a partial collision with the ecclesiastical world, and no collision with the civil world. Whereas the primitive 'offense of the cross,' was a full collision with the highest authorities both ecclesiastical and civil. Where then shall the death-blow of the flesh fall on the Gentile world? We answer—on marriage. That is a civil as well as religious ordinance, performed by clergymen and magistrates, defended by religion and law, common to all sects, and universal in the world. On that point the 'offense of the cross' will be just what it was in the apostolic age on the ordinances of Judaism.

Note 3.—We admit that Christ and the apostles, with wise reference to the transitory necessities and hostile surroundings of the church of their time, and to the purpose of God to give the Gentiles a dispensation of legal discipline, abstained from pushing the war against worldly institutions to the overthrow of marriage. Yet we insist that they left on record *principles* which go to the subversion of *all* worldly ordinances, and that the design of God was and is, that, at the end of the times of the Gentiles, the church should carry out those principles to their legitimate results.

PROPOSITION XII.—The law of marriage is the same in kind with the Jewish law concerning meats and drinks and holy days, of which Paul said that they were 'contrary to us, and were taken out of the way, being nailed to the cross.' Col. 2: 14. The plea in favor of the worldly system of sexual intercourse, that it is not arbitrary but founded in nature, will not bear investigation. All experience testifies, (the theory of the novels to the contrary notwithstanding,) that sexual love is not naturally restricted to pairs. Second marriages are contrary to the one-love theory, and yet are often the happiest marriages. Men and women find universally, (however the fact may be concealed,) that their susceptibility to love is not burnt out by one honey-moon, or satisfied by one lover. On the contrary, the secret history of the human heart will bear out the assertion that it is capable of loving any number of times and any number of persons, and that the more it loves the more it can love. This is the law of nature, thrust out of sight, and condemned by common consent, and yet secretly known to all. There is no occasion to find fault with it. Variety is, in the nature of things, as beautiful and useful in love as in eating and drinking. The one-love theory is the exponent, not of simple experience in love, but of the 'green-eyed monster,' jealousy. It is not the loving heart, but the greedy *claimant* of the loving heart, that sets up the popular doctrine that one only can be truly loved.

Note 1.—It is true, and an important truth, that in a right spiritual medium, the law of affinity may bring about special pairing ; i. e., that each individual may find a mate whose nature best matches his own, and whom of course he will love most. But this truth, confessedly, is no barrier to friendly relations and common conversation with others; and in the nature of things, it is no more a barrier to love and sexual intercourse with others.

Note 2.—There is undoubtedly a law of dualty in love indicated in all nature, and suggested in the creation of the first pair. Indeed this law takes its rise from the constitution of God himself, who is dual—the Father and the Son—in whose image man was made, male and female, and of whose nature the whole creation is a reflection. But the question is, how does this law operate in such a multiplex body as the church of Christ? Does it exhaust itself on the petty business of joining individual *persons* in pairs, or is its main force directed to the establishment of the

great dualty between the whole of one sex and the whole of the other?
There is dualty in a dancing party.   All that is done in the complex
movements of the whole company may be summed up in this: Man dances
with woman; but this general dualty is consistent with unlimited interchange of personal partnerships.   We cannot fairly infer anything in favor
of restricting sexual intercourse to pairs, from the fact that only two persons were created; for we might just as well infer from that fact that conversation and every other mode of intercourse ought to be restricted to pairs.
Adam in the garden had nobody to converse with but Eve, but this is no
reason why a man should talk with no body but his wife.   We maintain that
in the body of Christ, *universal* unity is the main point; and that the dualty
between all men and all women, overrides all inferior dualties.   For example, suppose a man, A, is married to a woman, B; and a man, C, to a
woman, D.   Our position is, that in Christ the union of the whole four is
first in importance, and the union of the pairs is secondary.   We say that
it is not enough that A is married to B, making the dual unit A B; and
C to D, making the dual unit C D; but that the unit A B ought also to
be married to the unit C D, making the quadruple unit A B C D.   And
we say further, that in the approach and marriage of the pair A B, to the
pair C D, it is the dictate of the law of dualty, and the self-evident demand
of nature, that the man of each pair should face the woman of the other.

Illustration.—In the figure an-
nexed, let the whole triangle ACE
represent Christ; then the triangles AED and ACD may represent
two generic churches in Christ, as
the Primitive and Gentile, or the
heavenly and the visible churches ;
the triangles AFD and EFD may

represent two nations in the church AED; and the triangles ABD
and CBD, two nations in the church ACD.   Let the eight triangles,
made by the union of the triangles 1 and 2, 3 and 4, 5 and 6, &c., be pairs
of male and female; and let the sixteen single triangles, 1, 2, 3, 4, 5, &c.,
be individual persons.   Here there are five sorts of interests to be cared
for : 1st, the interests of individuals; 2d, those of pairs; 3d, those of nations ; 4th, those of churches; 5th, those of Christ.   In what order shall
they be estimated ?   In the world the interests of individuals stand first,
of pairs second, and so on, the interests of Christ being last.   In a true
state this order is inverted.   The interests of Christ stand first, because
they include and are the sum of all other interests.   The unity of Christ
is more important, and therefore more sacred, than the individuality of
persons, the union of individuals in pairs, the union of pairs in nations, or
the union of nations in churches.   So throughout the series, the more
comprehensive unities take precedence of those that are less: the unity of

the generic churches is more important than that of nations; the unity of nations than that of pairs, &c. It may be seen also by this illustration, how the law of dualty is preserved in complexity. Each pair constitutes a triangular unit like each individual. Each union of pairs, as of 1 and 2 with 15 and 16, constitutes a dual unit of the same original form. Each union of nations, as of ABD with CBD, constitutes a similar dual unit. And the union of the two churches constitutes the universal dual unit, or body of Christ.

PROPOSITION XIII.—The law of marriage 'worketh wrath.' 1. It provokes to secret adultery, actual or of the heart.— 2. It ties together unmatched natures. 3. It sunders matched natures. 4. It gives to sexual appetite only a scanty and monotonous allowance, and so produces the natural vices of poverty, contraction of taste, and stinginess or jealousy. 5. It makes no provision for the sexual appetite at the very time when that appetite is the strongest. By the custom of the world, marriage, in the average of cases, takes place at about the age of twenty-four : whereas puberty commences at the age of fourteen. For ten years, therefore, and that in the very flush of life, the sexual appetite is starved. This law of society bears hardest on females, because they have less opportunity of choosing their time of marriage than men. This discrepancy between the marriage system and nature, is one of the principal sources of the peculiar diseases of women, of prostitution, masturbation, and licentiousness in general.

Note.—The only hopeful scheme of Moral Reform, is one which will bring the sexes together according to the demands of nature. The desire of the sexes is a stream ever running. If it is dammed up, it will break out irregularly and destructively. The only way to make it safe and useful, is to give it a free natural channel. Or to vary the illustration, the attractions of male and female are like positive and negative electricities. In equilibrium, they are quiet. Separate them, and they become turbulent: Prostitution, masturbation, and obscenity in general, are injurious eruptions, incident to unnatural separations of the male and female elements. Reform, in order to be effectual, must base itself on the principle of restoring and preserving equilibrium by free intercourse. Even in the world it is known that the mingling of the sexes to a certain extent, is favorable to purity ; and that sexual isolation, as in colleges, monasteries, &c., breeds salacity and obscenity. A system of complex-marriage, which shall match the demands of nature, both as to time and variety, will open the prison doors to the victims both of marriage and celibacy: to those in married life who are starved, and those who are oppressed by lust; to those who are tied to uncongenial natures, and those who are separated from their natural mates;—to those in the unmarried state who are withered by neglect, diseased by unnatural abstinence, or plunged into prostitution and self-pollution, by desires which find no lawful channel.

CHAPTER III.

Showing that Death is to be abolished in the Kingdom of Heaven, and that, to this end, there must be a restoration of true relations between the Sexes.

PROPOSITION XIV.—The kingdom of God on earth is destined to abolish death.   1 Cor. 15: 24—26.   Isaiah 25: 8.

Note.—The resurrection of Christ is the original factor, by the involution of which the resurrection of all other men is to be effected. Assuming that the resurrection of mankind is divided into two acts, and that one of these (the first resurrection) came to pass at the Second Coming, in A. D. 70, and that the other (which is the general resurrection) is yet future, (which propositions we have elsewhere established,) it is evident that we have, in the past, two matter-of-fact specimens of the nature of the resurrection, from which we must form our conclusions concerning the resurrection that is to come. As we call the resurrection of Christ the original factor, so (availing ourselves further of mathematical terms) we may say that the resurrection at the Second Coming was the *second power*, and that the coming resurrection will be the *third power*, of the resurrection of Christ. It is, in a certain sense, Christ's own body that is rising through all these resurrections. First, his personal body arose; then his corporate body, the Primitive church; and finally will be raised his completed, universal body. Now, whatever essential elements we find in the original factor, and in its second power, will also be found, we may be sure, in its third power. What then, in the first place, are the essential elements of the resurrection of Christ? We may take for an answer this Scripture: '*Thou wilt not leave my soul in Hades, nor suffer thine Holy One to see corruption.*' (Acts 2: 31.) The fact answering to this language in Christ's case was, the redemption of his soul *and* body from the power of death. In the next place we inquire, What were the elements of the resurrection at the Second Coming? The answer we find in the following announcements from the writings of Paul: '*We shall not all sleep,* [i. e., at the coming of the Lord, then at hand,] *but we shall all be changed. . . . The dead shall be raised incorruptible, and we shall be changed. . . If we be-*

lieve *that Jesus died and rose again, even so them also which sleep in Jesus, will God bring* [i. e., raise up] *with him. . . The dead in Christ shall rise first; then we which are alive and remain shall be* [*changed and*] *caught up,*' &c. 1 Cor. 15: 51, and 1 Thess. 4: 14. Observe, Paul reasons, as we do, from the elements of the original factor, and thence deduces two results, corresponding to the two facts which we have noted in Christ's resurrection, viz., *the return of the dead from Hades, corresponding to the redemption of Christ's soul; and the immortalization of the living, corresponding to the revival of Christ's body.* These anticipations became facts at the Second Coming, in A. D. 70. We are bound, then, in anticipating the final resurrection, or the resurrection of Christ, carried to its third power, to expect the same two elements, i. e., a complete victory over death in its two-fold power over the soul and over the body—against the dead and against the living; and as in this final victory the *world* is to be delivered up to Christ, (which was not the fact at the first resurrection,) *the redemption of soul and body from the power of death must be expected as a universal fact in this world;* which fact is indeed expressly predicted in the following glorious words of Isaiah: "In this mountain shall the Lord of hosts make unto all people a feast of fat things, a feast of wines on the lees; of fat things full of marrow, of wines on the lees well refined. And he will destroy in this mountain the face of the covering cast over all people, and the vail that is spread over all nations. HE WILL SWALLOW UP DEATH IN VICTORY; *and the Lord God will wipe away tears from off all faces; and the rebuke of his people shall he take away from off all the earth: for the Lord hath spoken it.*" Isaiah 25: 6: 8.

PROPOSITION XV.—The abolition of death is to be the *last* triumph of the kingdom of heaven; and the subjection of all other powers to Christ, must go before it. 1 Cor. 15: 24—26. Isaiah 33: 22—24.

Note 1.—This proposition can be shown to be rational as well as scriptural. The body cannot be saved from disease and death till Christ has control of the powers which determine the conditions of the body. The powers of law and custom, organizing society, determine the conditions of the body. For instance, the present form of society compels the mass of mankind to drag out life in excessive labor—a condition inconsistent with the welfare of the body. Before Christ can save the body, then, he must 'put down all [present] authority and rule,' and have power to organize society anew. A physician cannot cure diseases generated in a pestilential dungeon, while the patient remains there. The marriage system is a part of the machinery of present society, which seriously affects the conditions of the body, as appears in Proposition xiii. and Note, and as will appear further hereafter. Christ must, therefore, have control of this department,

and arrange sexual conditions according to the genius of his own kingdom, before he can push his conquests to victory over death. Whoever
has well studied the causes of human maladies, will be sure that Christ, in
undertaking to restore man to Paradise and immortality, will set up his
kingdom first of all, in the bed-chamber and the nursery.

Note 2.—This proposition gives a sufficient answer to those who insist
that the resurrection of the body must *go before* the social revolutions
which we propose. These revolutions are the very means by which the
resurrection power is to be let in upon the world. It might as ration-
ally be said that the snows of winter must not melt till the grass has
grown, or that the clods over the dead must not be broken up till the
dead have come forth from their graves, as that the institutions of this
world must not be abolished till the resurrection of the body is finished.
It is true that, as life works legitimately from within outward, the institutions of the world ought not to be broken up till holiness is established
in the heart, and moral discipline has advanced to maturity; i. e., till
all things are ready for the resurrection of the body. The shell of the
young bird ought not to be broken, till the life of the bird itself is sufficient to make the breach. Yet in the order of nature, the shell bursts
before the bird comes forth: so the breaking up of the fashion of the
world precedes the resurrection of the body.

Note 3.—The interests of human nature may be divided into three
classes—those of the soul, of the body, and of the estate. The rulers of this
world corresponding to these three classes of interests, are the clergy, the
doctors, and the lawyers. Christ must supplant all these rulers and take
their powers into his hands, before he can give man the redemption of the
body. It is not enough that his kingdom should be emancipated from the
priests. This may give redemption to the soul; but so long as the body
remains in the hands of the doctor, and the estate in the hands of the lawyer, it cannot be said that ' the Lord is our judge, the Lord is our law-
giver, the Lord is our king;' for ' other Lords besides him have dominion
over us;' and it is only when he is our only ruler that sickness and death
are to cease. See Isaiah 26 : 13, 14, and comp. ver. 19; also Isaiah 33: 22,
and comp. ver. 24.

PROPOSITION XVI.—The restoration of true relations between the sexes, is a matter second in importance only to the
reconciliation of man to God. The distinction of male and
female is that which makes man the image of God, i. e. the
image of the Father and the Son. Gen. 1: 27. The relation
of male and female was the first social relation. Gen. 2: 22.
It is therefore the root of all other social relations. The
derangement of this relation was the first result of the original

breach with God. Gen. 3: 7; comp. 2: 25. Adam and Eve were, at the beginning, in open, fearless, spiritual fellowship, first with God, and secondly, with each other. Their transgression produced two corresponding alienations, viz., first, an alienation from God, indicated by their fear of meeting him, and their hiding themselves among the trees of the garden; and, secondly, an alienation from each other, indicated by their shame at their nakedness, and their hiding themselves from each other by clothing. These were the two great manifestations of original sin—the only manifestations presented to notice in the inspired record of the apostasy. The first thing then to be done, in an attempt to redeem man and reörganize society, is to bring about reconciliation with God; and the second thing is to bring about a true union of the sexes. In other words, religion is the first subject of interest, and sexual morality the second, in the great enterprise of establishing the kingdom of God on earth.

Note 1.—Bible Communists are operating in this order. Their main work, from 1834 to 1846, was to develop the religion of the New Covenant, and establish union with God. The second work, in which they are now specially engaged, is the laying the foundation of a new state of society, by developing the true theory of sexual morality.

Note 2.—The functions of the two churches, Jewish and Gentile, correspond to the two breaches to be repaired. It was the special function of the Primitive church (which was the interior or soul-church) to break up the worldly *ecclesiastical* system, and establish true religion, thus opening full communication with God. It is the special function of the present or body-church, (availing itself first of the work of the Primitive church, by union with it, and a re-development of its theology,) to break up the *social* system of the world, and establish true external order by the reconciliation of the sexes.

Note 3.—We may criticise the system of the Fourierists, thus: The chain of evils which holds humanity in ruin, has four links, viz., 1st, a breach with God; (Gen. 3: 8;) 2d, a disruption of the sexes, involving a special curse on woman; (Gen. 3: 16;) 3d, the curse of oppressive labor, bearing specially on man: (Gen. 3: 17—19;) 4th, the reign of disease and death. (Gen. 3: 22—24.) These are all inextricably complicated with each other. The true scheme of redemption begins with reconciliation with God, proceeds first to a restoration of true relations between the sexes, then to a reform of the industrial system, and ends with victory over

death. Fourierism has no eye to the final victory over death, defers attention to the religious question and the sexual question till some centuries
hence, and confines itself to the rectifying of the industrial system.   In
other words, Fourierism neither begins at the beginning, nor looks to the
end of the chain, but fastens its whole interest on the third link, neglect-
ing two that precede it, and ignoring that which follows it.   The sin-sys-
tem, the marriage-system, the work-system, and the death-system, are all
one, and must be abolished together.   Holiness, free love, association in
labor, and immortality, constitute the chain of redemption, and must come
together in their true order.

Note 4.—N. B. From what precedes, it is evident that any attempt to revolutionize sexual morality before settlement with
God, is out of order.   Holiness must go before Free Love.   Bible
Communists are not responsible for the proceedings of those who
meddle with the sexual question, before they have laid the foundation of true faith and union with God.

Proposition XVII.—Dividing the sexual relation into two
branches, the amative and propagative, the amative or love-
relation is first in importance, as it is in the order of nature.
God made woman because 'he saw it was *not good for man
to be alone;'* (Gen. 2: 18;) i. e. for social, not primarily for
propagative purposes.   Eve was called Adam's 'help-meet.'
In the whole of the specific account of the creation of woman,
she is regarded as his companion, and her maternal office is
not brought into view. Gen. 2: 18–25.   Amativeness was necessarily the first social affection developed in the garden of Eden.
The second commandment of the eternal law of love,—'thou
shalt love thy neighbor as thyself'—had amativeness for its
first channel; for Eve was at first Adam's only neighbor.—
Propagation, and the affections connected with it, did not
commence their operation during the period of innocence.—
After the fall, God said to the woman,—'I will greatly multiply thy sorrow and thy conception;' from which it is to be
inferred that in the original state, conception would have been
comparatively infrequent.

Note 1.—It is true that God made provision for propagation, in the organization of the first pair, and expressed his design that they should
multiply. Gen. 1: 28. This opposes the Shaker theory. But it is clear
that if innocence had continued, propagation would have been much less

frequent than it is now, and would have been altogether secondary to amativeness.

Note 2.—Because the power of propagation resides in sexual commerce, and forms its visible concrete consequence, it has been assumed generally that therefore propagation is the chief end and object of the sexual constitution. Nature however indicates in various ways that pleasure, or amative social union, stands before propagation, as the superior function. A melon, for example, is created full of seeds, and possesses an extensive power of propagation. Its main bulk, however, surrounding the seed department, (as in most esculent fruits,) is adapted to be eaten. Here are two functious or points of value, one relating to the seed, the other to the pulp—one representing propagation. the other enjoyment. Which is the primary? Evidently the latter; for we feel that the chief end and value of the fruit is realized when it is eaten and converted to.human enjoyment, even though its seeds are thrown away, and its propagative destiny is left unregarded. Those who make everything turn on the principle of propagative use, to be consistent, should avoid consuming any more fruit than is needed to seed the earth with fruit-plants.

Note 3.—If the proposition that personal interests take precedence of propagation, (as the cause is worth more than its effects,) is not self-evident, we may demonstrate it thus; Let A, B, C, D, &c., represent a propagative series, A being the father of B, and B of C, &c. Now if we suppose it to be the chief end of man to propagate instead of making the most of himself, we carry forward the end for which A lives, into B, his offspring. But it does not rest there: for B again lives for the sake of begetting and rearing C; and then C's mission is to produce D, and so on through the alphabet. Now as the series may be endless, it is evident that on this principle no positive value will ever be attained as the end of A's existence or of that of his descendants. All that can be said of the process, is, that A lives for the sake of producing the producer of the producer of the producer—of what? Nothing; because this term *producer* extends on and on, *ad infinitum.* The only satisfactory view is that the chief value of every man is in himself, as the chief value of the apple is in its eatable pulp, and not in its power of propagation.

Note 4.—Naturalists say that in all organic life, the propagative tendency is *inversely as the value of the species;* i. e., the meanest forms of life, like thistles and musquitoes, are luxuriant in multiplying seed, and sending abroad missionaries, while all valuable plants and animals have moderate propagative tendencies, spending their strength principally in perfecting their own usefulness.

PROPOSITION XVIII.—The amative part of the sexual relation, (separate from the propagative,) is eminently favorable to life. It is not a *source* of life, (as some would make it,) but it

is the first and best *distributive* of life. Adam and Eve, in
their original state, derived their life from God. Gen. 2: 7.
As God is a dual being—the Father and the Son—and man
was made in his image; a dual life passed from God to man.
Adam was the channel specially of the life of the Father, and
Eve of the life of the Son. Amativeness was the natural
agency of the distribution and mutual action of these two
forms of life. In this primitive position of the sexes, (which
is the position of the sexes in Christ,) each reflects upon the
other the love of God; each excites and develops the divine
action in the other. Thus amativeness is to life, as sunshine
to vegetation.

Note 1.—By man's fall from God, he came into a state (like that of the
other animals) of dependence on the fruits of the earth for life; i. e., he
became 'dust,' and commenced his return to 'dust.' Gen. 3: 19. At the
same time the alienation of the sexes took place. So that in the fallen
state both the source and the distribution of life are deranged and ob-
structed. Yet even in this state, love between the sexes, separate from the
curse of propagation, (as in courtship,) develops the highest vigor and
beauty of human nature.

Note 2.—The complexity of the human race does not alter the relation
of amativeness to life, as defined in the foregoing proposition. If Adam
and Eve, in their original union with God and with each other, had become
complex by propagation, still the life and love of the Father and the Son
would have been reflected by the whole of one sex upon the whole of the
other. The image of God would have remained a dualty, complex, yet re-
taining the conditions of the original dualty. Amative action between
the sexes would have been like the galvanic action between alternate plates
of copper and zinc. As the series of plates is extended, the original action, though it remains the same in nature, becomes more and more intense. So the love between the Father and the Son, in the complexity of
Christ's body, will be developed with an intensity proportioned to the extent of alternation and conjunction of male and female. Victory over
death will be the result of the action of an extensive battery of this kind.

Note 3.—Sexual intercourse, apart from the propagative act, (and it will
appear hereafter that the two may be separated,) is the appropriate external expression of amativeness, and is eminently favorable to life. The
contact and unity of male and female bodies, develops and distributes the
two kinds of life which in equilibrium constitute perfect vitality. Mere re-
ciprocal communication of vital heat is healthful, (Eccles. 4: 11,) and communication between male and female is more perfect than between persons

of the same sex. 1 Kings 1: 1–4. The principle involved in the doctrine of 'laying on of hands,' (which was a fundamental doctrine of the Primitive church, and was brought into practice in the communication of spiritual life both to soul and body,) is, that not only animal life, but the Spirit of God, passes from one to another by bodily contact. This principle is not restricted to mere literal 'laying on of hands.' Paul revived Eutychus, by falling on him and embracing him. Acts 20: 9---12. So Elijah stretched himself upon the child; (1 Kings 17: 21;) 'and Elisha lay upon the child, and put his mouth upon his mouth, and his eyes upon his eyes, and his hands upon his hands, till the flesh of the child waxed warm,' &c. 2 Kings 4: 34. The specific method of bodily contact is not essential to the principle, but may be varied indefinitely. It is safe to affirm that the more intimate and perfect the contact, the greater will be the effect, other things being equal. On this principle, sexual intercourse is in its nature the most perfect method of 'laying on of hands,' and under proper circumstances may be the most powerful external agency of communicating life to the body, and even the Spirit of God to the mind and heart.

Note 4.—We see how foolish they are who think and speak of amativeness and sexual intercourse as contemptible, and in their nature unclean and debasing. Such persons not only dishonor God's creation, but despise that part of human nature which is the noblest of all, except that which communicates with God. They profane the very sanctuary of the affections—the first and best channel of the life and love of God.

Note 5.—The familiar principle that the abuse of a thing is no discredit to its use, and that the destructiveness of an element, when abused, is the measure of its usefulness when rightly managed, applies to amativeness and its expression. If amativeness is a fire, which under the devil's administration burns houses, why may it not under God's administration prepare food, warm dwellings, and drive steamboats? If it is Satan's agency of death, why may it not be God's agency of resurrection?

PROPOSITION XIX.—The propagative part of the sexual relation is in its nature the *expensive* department. 1. While amativeness keeps the capital stock of life circulating between two, propagation introduces a third partner. 2. The propagative act, i. e. the emission of the seed, is a drain on the life of man, and when habitual, produces disease. 3. The infirmities and vital expenses of woman during the long period of pregnancy, waste her constitution. 4. The awful agonies of child-birth heavily tax the life of woman. 5. The cares of the nursing period bear heavily on woman. 6. The cares of both parents, through the period of the childhood of their offspring, are many and burdensome. 7. The labor of man is greatly increased by the necessity of providing for children. A portion of these expenses would undoubtedly have been curtailed, if human nature had remained in its original integrity, and will be, when it is restored. But it is still self-evident, that the birth of children, viewed either as a vital or a mechanical operation, is in its nature expensive ; and the fact that multiplied conception was imposed as a curse, indicates that it was so regarded by the Creator.

Note 1.—Amativeness being the profitable part, and propagation the expensive part of the sexual relation, it is evident that a true balance between them is essential to the interests of the vital economy. If expenses exceed income, bankruptcy ensues. After the fall, sin and shame curtailed amativeness, thus diminishing the profitable department; and the curse increased propagation, thus enlarging the expensive department. Death, i. e. vital bankruptcy, is the law of the race in its fallen condition ; and it results more from this derangement of the sexual economy, than from any other cause, except the disruption from God. It is the expression of the disproportion of amativeness to propagation—or of life to its expenses ; each generation dies in giving life to its successor.

Note 2.—The actual proportion of the amative to the propagative, in the world, may probably be estimated fairly by comparing the time of courtship (which is the limit of the novels) with the breeding part of married life ; or by comparing the momentary pleasures of ordinary sexual intercourse with the protracted woes of pregnancy, birth, nursing and breeding.

Note 3.—The grand problem which must be solved before redemption can be carried forward to immortality, is this:—*How can the benefits of amativeness be secured and increased, and the expenses of propagation be reduced to such limits as life can afford?* The human mind has labored much on this problem. Shakerism is an attempt to solve it. Ann Lee's attention, however, was confined to the latter half of it—the reduction of expenses; (of which her own sufferings in child-birth gave her a strong sense;) and for the sake of stopping propagation she prohibited the union of the sexes—thus shutting off the profitable as well as the expensive part of the sexual relation. This is cutting the knot— not untying it. Robert Dale Owen's 'Moral Physiology' is another attempted solution of the grand problem. He insists that sexual intercourse is of some value by itself, and not merely as a bait to propagation. He proposes therefore to limit propagation, and retain the privilege of sexual intercourse, by the practice of withdrawing previous to the emission of the seed, after Onan's fashion. Gen. 38: 9. This method, it will be observed, is unnatural, and even

more wasteful of life, so far as the man is concerned, than ordinary practice ; since it gives more freedom to desire, by shutting off the propagative
consequences. The same may be said of various French methods. The
system of producing abortions, is a still more unnatural and destructive
method of limiting propagation, without stopping sexual intercourse. A
satisfactory solution of the grand problem, must propose a method that
can be shown to be natural, healthy for both sexes, favorable to amativeness, and effectual in its control of propagation. Such a solution will be
found in what follows.

CHAPTER IV.

*Showing how the Sexual Function is to be redeemed, and true
relations between the sexes restored.*

PROPOSITION XX.—The amative and propagative functions
of the sexual organs are distinct from each other, and may be
separated practically. They are confounded in the world,
both in the theories of physiologists and in universal practice.
The amative function is regarded merely as a bait to the propagative, and is merged in it. The sexual organs are called
'organs of reproduction,' or 'organs of generation,' but not organs of love or organs of union. But if amativeness is, as we
have seen, the first and noblest of the social affections, and if
the propagative part of the sexual relation was originally secondary, and became paramount by the subversion of order in
the fall, we are bound to raise the amative office of the sexual
organs into a distinct and paramount function. It is held in
the world, that the sexual organs have two distinct functions,
viz., the urinary and the propagative. We affirm that they
have *three*—the urinary, the propagative, and the amative, i. e.,
they are conductors, first of the urine, secondly of the semen,
and thirdly of the social magnetism. And the amative
is as distinct from the propagative, as the propagative
is from the urinary. In fact, strictly speaking, the organs of
propagation are *physiologically* distinct from the organs of
union in both sexes. The testicles are the organs of reproduction in the male, and the uterus in the female. These

are distinct from the organs of union. The sexual conjunction of male and female, no more necessarily involves the
discharge of the semen than of the urine. The discharge of
the semen, instead of being the main act of sexual intercourse,
properly so called, is really the sequel and termination of it.
Sexual intercourse, pure and simple, is the conjunction of the
organs of union, and the interchange of magnetic influences,
or conversation of spirits, through the medium of that conjunction. The communication from the seminal vessels to the
uterus, which constitutes the propagative act, is distinct from,
subsequent to, and not necessarily connected with, this intercourse. (On the one hand, the seminal discharge can be volun-
tarily witheld in sexual connection ; and on the other, it can
be produced without sexual connection, as it is in masturbation. This latter fact demonstrates that the discharge of the
semen and the pleasure connected with it, is not essentially
social, since it can be produced in solitude ; it is a personal
and not a dual affair. This, indeed, is evident from a physio-
logical analysis of it. The pleasure of the act is not produced
by contact and interchange of life with the female, but by the
action of the seminal fluid on certain internal nerves of the
male organ. The appetite and that which satisfies it, are both
within the man, and of course the pleasure is personal, and
may be obtained without sexual intercourse.) We insist then
that the amative function—that which consists in a simple
union of persons, making ' of twain one flesh,' and giving a
medium of magnetic and spiritual interchange—is a distinct
and independent function, as superior to the reproductive as
we have shown amativeness to be to propagation.

Note 1.—We may strengthen the argument of the preceding proposition
by an analogy. The *mouth* has three distinct functions, viz., those of
breathing, eating, and speaking. Two of these, breathing and eating, are
purely physical; and these we have in common with the brutes. The third
function, that of speaking, is social, and subservient to the intellectual and
spiritual. In this we rise above the brutes. They are destitute of it except in a very inferior degree. So, the two primary functions of the sexual organs—the urinary and reproductive—are physical, and we have them

in common with the brutes. The third, viz., the amative, is social, and subservient to the spiritual. In this again we rise above the brutes.— They have it only as a bait to the reproductive. As speech, the distinctive glory of man, is the superior function of the mouth, so the amative office of the sexual organs is their superior function, and that which gives man a position above the brutes.

Note 2.—Man's superiority to the brutes is read in his continual advance in the conquest of nature. The brutes stand still; men reflect, energize, and conquer. The seeds of the final supremacy over nature lie in the full subjection of man's own body to his intelligent will. There are already an abundance of familiar facts showing the influence of education and direct discipline in developing the powers of the body. We see men every day, who by attention and pains-taking investigation and practice in some mechanical art, have gained a power over their muscles, for certain purposes, which to the mere natural man would be impossible or miraculous. In music, the great violinists and pianists are examples.— All the voluntary faculties, are known to come under the power of education, and the human will is found able to express itself in the motions of the body, to an extent and perfection that is in proportion to the pains-taking and discipline that are applied. So far as the department of voluntary, outward habits is concerned, the influence of will and education to control the body is universally admitted. But there is a step further. Investigation and experience are now ready to demonstrate the power of the will over what have been considered and called the *involuntary* processes of the body. The mind can take control of them certainly to a great extent, and while it is not yet shown to what extent, neither is it apparent that there are any limits whatever in this direction. All the later discoveries point to the conclusion, that there are strictly no *involuntary* departments in the human system, but that every part falls appropriately and in fact within the dominion of mind, spirit and will. It has been proved by abundant experiments that control can be established over the respiratory organs. Dyspepsia has been cured by a voluntary system of attention to and regulation of the method of breathing. Consumption has been cured by a determined suppression of coughing. So also the involuntary operations of the stomach and bowels have been found controlable. The tendency to vomiting in sea-sickness, and the opposite inclination in cholera symptoms, have been, by a judicious exercise of the will, repeatedly broken up. Finally, we now assert that the propagative crisis, so far from being an involuntary part of sexual intercourse, is a matter clearly within the province of the will—subject to enlightened voluntary control.

Note 3.—Here is a method of controlling propagation, that is natural, healthy, favorable to amativeness, and effectual. First, It is *natural.* The useless expenditure of seed certainly is not natural. God cannot have designed that men should sow seed by the way-side, where they do not expect it to grow, or in the same field where seed has already been sown, and is growing; and yet such is the practice of men in ordinary sexual intercourse. They sow seed habitually where they do not *wish* it to grow. This is wasteful of life, and cannot be natural. So far the Shakers and Grahamites are right. Yet it is equally manifest that the natural instinct of our nature demands frequent congress of the sexes, not for propagative, but for social and spiritual purposes. It results from these opposite indications, that simple congress of the sexes, *without the propagative crisis*, is the order of nature for the gratification of ordinary amative instincts; and that the act of propagation should be reserved for its legitimate occasions, when conception is intended. The idea that sexual intercourse, pure and simple, is impossible or difficult, and therefore not natural, is contradicted by the experience of many. Abstinence from masturbation is impossible or difficult, where habit has made it a second nature; and yet no one will say that habitual masturbation is natural. So abstinence from the propagative part of sexual intercourse may seem impracticable to depraved natures, and yet be perfectly natural and easy to persons properly trained to chastity. Our method simply proposes the subordination of the flesh to the spirit, teaching men to seek principally the elevated spiritual pleasures of sexual intercourse, and to be content with them in their general intercourse with women, restricting the more sensual part to its proper occasions. This is certainly natural and easy to spiritual men, however difficult it may be to the sensual.

Secondly, this method is *healthy*. In the first place, it secures woman from the curses of involuntary and undesirable procreation; and secondly, it stops the drain of life on the part of man. This cannot be said of Owen's system, or any other method that merely prevents the *propagative effects* of the emission of the seed, and not the emission itself.

Thirdly, this method is *favorable to amativeness*. Owen can only say of his method that it does not *much diminish* the pleasure of sexual intercourse; but we can say of ours, that it *vastly increases* that pleasure. Ordinary sexual intercourse (in which the amative and propagative functions are confounded) is a momentary affair, terminating in exhaustion and disgust. If it begins in the spirit, it soon ends in the flesh; i. e., the amative, which is spiritual, is drowned in the propagative, which is sensual. The exhaustion which follows, naturally breeds self-reproach and shame, and this leads to dislike and concealment of the sexual organs, which contract disagreeable associations from the fact that they are the instruments of pernicious excess. This undoubtedly is the philosophy of the origin of shame after the fall. Adam and Eve first sunk the spiritual in the sensual, in eating the forbidden fruit; and then, having lost the true

balance of their natures, they sunk the spiritual in the sensual in their intercourse with each other, by pushing prematurely beyond the amative to
the propagative, and so became ashamed, and began to look with an evil
eye on the instruments of their folly. On the same principle we may account for the process of ' cooling off' which takes place between lovers after
marriage, and often ends in indifference and disgust. Exhaustion and self-
reproach make the eye evil not only toward the instruments of excess, but
toward the person who tempts to it. In contrast with all this, lovers who
use their sexual organs simply as the servants of their spiritual natures,
abstaining from the propagative act, except when procreation is intended,
may enjoy the highest bliss of sexual fellowship for any length of time, and
from day to day, without satiety or exhaustion; and thus marriage life
may become permanently sweeter than courtship, or even the honey-moon.

Fourthly, this method of controlling propagation is *effectual.* The habit
of making sexual intercourse a quiet affair, like conversation, restricting
the action of the organs to such limits as are necessary to the avoidance
of the sensual crisis, can easily be established, and then there is no risk
of conception without intention.

Note 4.—Ordinary sexual intercourse, i. e., the performance of the propagative act, without the intention of procreation, is properly to be classed
with masturbation. The habit in the former case is less liable to become
besotted and ruinous, than in the latter, simply because a woman is less
convenient than the ordinary means of masturbation. It must be admitted, also, that the amative affection favorably modifies the sensual act
to a greater extent in sexual commerce than in masturbation. But this is
perhaps counterbalanced by the cruelty of forcing or risking undesired conception, which attends sexual commerce, and does not attend masturbation.

Note 5.—Our theory, separating the amative from the propagative, not
only relieves us of involuntary and undesirable procreation, but opens the
way for *scientific* propagation. We are not opposed, after the Shaker fashion, or even after Owen's fashion, to the increase of population. We believe
that the order to 'multiply' attached to the race in its original integrity,
and that propagation, rightly conducted, and kept within such limits as
life can fairly afford, is the next blessing to sexual love. But we are opposed to *involuntary* procreation. A very large proportion of all children
born under the present system, are begotten contrary to the wishes of both
parents, and lie nine months in their mother's womb under their mother's
curse, or a feeling little better than a curse. Such children cannot be wel
organized. We are opposed to *excessive*, and of course oppressive procreation, which is almost universal. We are opposed to *random* procreation,
which is unavoidable in the marriage system. But we are in favor of *intelligent, well-ordered* procreation. The physiologists say that the race
cannot be raised from ruin till propagation is made a matter of science;

but they point out no way of making it so. True, propagation is controlled and reduced to a science in the case of valuable domestic brutes; but marriage and fashion forbid any such system among human beings. We believe the time will come when involuntary and random propagation will cease, and when scientific combination will be applied to human generation as freely and successfully as it is to that of other animals. The way will be open for this, when amativeness can have its proper gratification without drawing after it procreation, as a necessary sequence. And at all events, we believe that good sense and benevolence will *very soon* sanction and enforce the rule, that women shall bear children only when they choose. They have the principal burdens of breeding to bear, and they, rather than men, should have their choice of time and circumstances, at least till science takes charge of the business.

Note 6.—The political economist will perhaps find in our discovery some help for the solution of the famous 'population question.' CAREY, and other American writers on political economy, seem to have exploded the old Malthusian doctrine that population necessarily outruns subsistence; but there is still a difficulty in the theoretical prospect of the world in regard to population, which they do not touch. Admitting that the best soils are yet in reserve, and that with the progress of intelligence, means of subsistence may for the present increase faster than population; it is nevertheless certain that the actual *area* of the earth is a limited thing, and it is therefore certain that if its population goes on doubling, as we are told, once in twenty-five years, a time must come at last when there will not be standing-room! Whether such a catastrophe is worth considering and providing for or not, we may be certain, that man, when he has grown wise enough to be worthy of his commission as Lord of nature, will be able to determine for himself what shall be the population of the earth, instead of leaving it to be determined by the laws that govern the blind passions of brutes.

Note 7.—The separation of the amative from the propagative, places amative sexual intercourse on the same footing with other ordinary forms of intercourse, such as conversation, kissing, shaking hands, embracing, &c. So long as the amative and propagative are confounded, sexual intercourse carries with it physical consequences which necessarily take it out of the category of mere social acts. If a man under the cover of a mere social call upon a woman, should leave in her apartments a child for her to breed and provide for, he would do a mean wrong. The call might be made without previous negotiation or agreement, but the sequel of the call—the leaving of the child—is a matter so serious that it is to be treated as a business affair, and not be done without good reason and agreement of the parties. But the man who under the cover of social intercourse, commits the propagative act, leaves his child with the woman in a meaner and more oppressive way, than if he should leave it full born in her apartments; for he imposes upon her not only the task of breeding and providing for it, but the sorrows and pains of pregnancy and child-birth. It is right that law, or at least public opinion, should frown on such proceedings even more than it does ; and it is not to be wondered at that women, to a considerable extent, look upon ordinary sexual intercourse with more dread than pleasure, regarding it as a stab at their life, rather than a joyful act of fellowship. But separate the amative from the propagative—let the act of fellowship stand by itself—and sexual intercourse becomes a purely social affair, the same in kind with other modes of kindly interchange, differing only by its superior intensity and beauty. Thus the most popular, if not the most serious objection to free love and sexual intercourse, is removed. The difficulty so often urged, of knowing to whom children belong in complex-marriage, will have no place in a community trained to keep the amative distinct from the propagative. Thus also the only plausible objection to amative intercourse between near relatives, founded on the supposed law of nature that ' breeding in and in' deteriorates offspring, (which law however was not recognized in Adam's family,) is removed ; since science may dictate in this case as in all others, in regard to propagation, and yet amativeness may be free.

Note 7.—In society trained in these principles, as propagation will become a science, so amative intercourse will have place among the 'fine arts.' Indeed it will take rank above music, painting, sculpture, &c. ; for it combines the charms and benefits of them all. There is as much room for cultivation of taste and skill in this department as in any.

Note 8.—The practice which we propose will advance civilization and refinement at railroad speed. The self-control, retention of life, and ascent out of sensualism, which must result from making freedom of love a bounty on the chastening of physical indulgence, will at once raise the race to new vigor and beauty, moral and physical. And the refining effects of sexual love (which are recognized more or less in the world) will be increased a thousand-fold, when sexual intercourse becomes a method of ordinary conversation, and each is married to all.

CHAPTER V.

Showing that Shame, instead of being one of the prime virtues, is a part of original Sin, and belongs to the Apostasy.

PROPOSITION XXI.—Sexual shame was the consequence of the fall, and is factitious and irrational. (Gen. 2: 25 ; comp. 3: 7.) Adam and Eve, while innocent, had no shame ; little

children have none; other animals have none. To be ashamed
of the sexual organs, is to be ashamed of God's workmanship.
To be ashamed of the sexual organs, is to be ashamed
of the most perfect instruments of love and unity. To be
ashamed of the sexual organs, is to be ashamed of the agencies
which gave us existence. To be ashamed of sexual conjunction, is to be ashamed of the image of the glory of God—the
physical symbol of life dwelling in life, which is the mystery
of the gospel. John 17: 21, &c.

Note 1.—One of the *sources* of shame is *personal isolation*, which was
the consequence of the victory of the flesh over the spirit, which took
place when Adam and Eve forsook the counsel of God. Their unity with
God and with each other was in their spiritual part. In the physical they
were two. When the physical, therefore, became paramount, as it did
when they sought blessing from fruit instead of from God, they became
consciously two. Then began evil-eyed *surveillance* on the one hand, and
morbid shrinking on the other. A man is not ashamed of his body before
his own eyes, but before the eyes of another. So Adam and Eve were not
ashamed so long as they were one; but when they became two, their eyes
were opened, and they became ashamed. Another source of shame is *sensual excess*, in the fall from amative interchange to propagative expense,
producing exhaustion, consciousness of uncontrolled and ruinous passion,
and consequent aversion to the instruments of the mischief. This cause
acts particularly on the male. (See Proposition xx., Note 3.) Another
cause of shame is found in the *woes of untimely and excessive child-bearing*, by which the sexual organs and offices contract odious associations.
This cause acts particularly on the female. After the sentiment of shame
(i. e. the sentiment which prompts to dishonor and to conceal the sexual
organs) is generated by these causes, *jealousy* falls in with it and strength-
ens it. The greedy lover is naturally a fierce friend of a sentiment which
secludes the charms of his mistress from all senses but his own. And
then custom, and finally law, elevates this spawn of corruption into a
virtue.

Note 2.—It is true that God, in the Mosaic law and in other ways, has
added to the strength of the shame-principle, by precepts directed against
lewdness. But it must be remembered that all such legislation is predi-
cated on a state of spiritual derangement, and its end is, not to restore the
patient, but to prevent him from destructive violence, even at the expense
of increasing his internal malady. Shame is a good strait-jacket for
crazy amativeness, and as such God has favored it. Adam and Eve first
began to make *flimsy aprons* for their nakedness, and God interposed and

made them *complete garments.* Gen. 3: 7, 21. But he did not thereby approbate the spiritual and moral condition which made garments necessary.

Note 3.—True modesty is a sentiment which springs not from aversion or indifference to the sexual organs and offices, but from a delicate and reverent appreciation of their value and sacredness. While the shrinking of shame is produced by a feeling that the sexual nature is vile and shameful, the shrinking of modesty is produced by the opposite feeling, that the sexual nature is too holy and glorious to be meddled with lightly. This healthful delicacy is valuable as a preservative, and increases the pleasure of love. Modesty and shame ought to be sundered, and shame ought to be banished from the company of virtue, though in the world it has stolen the very name of virtue.

Note 4.—Shame is the real source of the impression, which many persist in exalting into a serious theory, that sexual distinction and sexual offices have no place in heaven. Any one who has true modesty, as above defined, would sooner consent to the banishment of singing from heaven, than of sexual music. The impression referred to is too self-evidently absurd to be argued with to any great extent, and can be abolished only by abolishing shame from which it originates, and making men and women truly modest. From pure feelings, sensible theories will flow. The loathsome loathings of the debauchee in a state of reaction must not make theories of taste and pleasure for the innocent.

Note 5.—The aversion which many have to thought and conversation on the subject we are considering, is like the aversion of the irreligious to thought and conversation about God and eternity. As irreconciliation makes thought about God disagreeable, so the sentiment of shame, whether contracted by debauchery or by education and epidemic spiritual influence, makes thought, and especially new thought and free discussion about sexual matters, disagreeable. Under the influence of that sentiment the mind is evil-eyed, and not in condition to reason clearly and see purely.— In such cases a vital conversion from the spirit of shame to the spirit of true modesty, must go before intellectual emancipation.

Note 6.—That kind of taste which rises from the sentiment of shame, excludes such books as the Bible and Shakspeare from virtuous libraries. (Vide Dr. Webster's Bible, Dr. Humphrey's criticisms of Shakspeare, &c.)

Note 7.—That kind of moral reform which rises from the sentiment of shame, attempts a hopeless war with nature. Its policy is to prevent pruriency by keeping the mind in ignorance of sexual subjects; whilst nature is constantly thrusting those subjects upon the mind. Whoever would preserve the minds of the young in innocence by keeping them from 'polluting images,' must first of all carry moral reform into the barn-yard and among the flies.

Note 8.—The true way to purify the mind in its amative department, is
to let in the light; to elevate sexual love by marrying it to religion; to
clear away the vile, debasing associations which usually crowd around the
thoughts of the sexual organs and offices, and substitute true and beautiful associations. The union of the child with its mother in nursing, is
not base, but lovely and even sacred to the imagination. Sexual intercourse is as much more lovely and sacred, as we have seen amativeness to
be superior to propagation. Instead of thinking of our sexual nature in
connection with sensuality and vice and woe, it is just as easy, and much
truer to God and nature, to associate with it images of the garden of Eden,
of the holy of holies, of God and heaven, thoughts of purity and chaste affection, of joy unspeakable and full of glory. The eucharist is a symbol of
eating Christ's flesh and drinking his blood; (Luke 22: 19—24;) of a
union with him in which we dwell in him and he in us; (John 6: 56;)
whereby we become bone of his bone and flesh of his flesh; (Eph. 5: 30;)
and he comes in to us, and sups with us, and we with him. Rev. 3: 20. Is
not this a *marriage* supper? And is not sexual intercourse a more perfect symbol of it than eating bread and drinking wine? With pure hearts
and minds, we may approach the sexual union as the truest Lord's supper,
as an emblem and also a medium of the noblest worship of God and fellowship with the body of Christ. We may throw around it all the hallowed
associations which attach to the festivities and hospitalities of Christmas
or Thanksgiving. To sup with each other, is really less sensual than to
sup with roast-turkeys and chicken-pies. Such thoughts surely are better than the base imaginations of shame which envelop the whole sexual
department in filth and darkness, even in the minds of those who would
be thought intelligent and refined. The Bible constantly associates ideas
of heaven with sexual intercourse. Isaiah 62: 4, 5. Matt. 22: 2—4; 25:
1—12; Rev. 19: 7; 21: 2, 9, &c. The wisest of men expressed his taste
in a song of love.

Note 9.—Shame seeks to degrade sexual intercourse by calling it 'sensual and carnal.' We reply, conversation is 'sensual and carnal.' Speech, in
itself, is nothing but a wagging of the tongue (a carnal member) on the one
hand, and a consequent vibration of the tympanum and nerves of the ear on
the other. Yet speech is the medium of spiritual blessings and refined interchange. Music is 'sensual and carnal.' Eating and drinking are 'sensual and carnal,' &c. Things 'sensual and carnal' are not necessarily vile
and unprofitable, as may be seen in Rom. 15: 27, and 1 Cor. 9: 11. By
themselves they are of small value; and out of place, i. e., overlaying and
abusing the spiritual, they are diabolical; but in their place, as servants of
the spiritual, they are of great value. The senses are to the thoughts and
affections of the spirit, as chess-men to a chess-game. By themselves,
chess-men are trifles; and to play with them as children do, for their own
sake, would be frivolous and degrading; but as instruments of the compli-

cated thought and interest of a chess-game, they are not contemptible.— It is the ascetic and Manichean philosophy, not the Bible, that despises the senses and matter. Of all the pleasures of the senses, sexual intercourse is intrinsically the most spiritual and refined; for it is intercourse of human life with human life; whereas in every other sensual enjoyment, human life has intercourse with inanimate matter, or life inferior to itself. In the same sense as that in which sexual intercourse is 'sensual and carnal,' Peter's 'kiss of charity,' (1 Peter 5: 14,) which Paul calls 'holy,' (Rom. 16: 16, and 1 Cor. 16: 20,) and which both apostles enjoined, is 'sensual and carnal.' In the same sense, 'laying on of hands' is 'sensual and carnal,' &c.

CHAPTER VI.

Showing the bearings of the preceding views on Socialism, Political Economy, Manners and Customs, &c.

PROPOSITION XXII.—The foregoing principles concerning the sexual relation, open the way for Association. 1. They furnish *motives.* They apply to larger partnerships the same attractions as draw and bind together pairs in the worldly partnership of marriage. A Community-home in which each is married to all, and where love is honored and cultivated, will be as much more attractive than an ordinary home, even in the honey-moon, as the Community out-numbers a pair. A motive thus mighty is needed for the Association enterprise.— 2. These principles remove the principal *obstructions* in the way of Association. There is plenty of tendency to crossing love, and adultery, even in the system of isolated households. Association increases this tendency. Amalgamation of interests, frequency of interview, and companionship in labor, inevitably give activity and intensity to the social attractions in which amativeness is the strongest element. The tendency to extra-matrimonial love will be proportioned to the condensation of interests produced by any given form of Association; i. e., if the ordinary principles of exclusiveness are preserved, Association will be a worse school of temptation to unlawful love than the world is, in proportion to its social advantages. Love, in the exclusive form, has jealousy for its complement; and jealousy brings on strife and division. Association, therefore, if it retains one-love exclusiveness, contains the seeds of dissolution; and those seeds will be hastened to their harvest by the warmth of associate life. An association of States, with custom-house lines around each, is sure to be quarrelsome. The further States in that situation are apart, and the more their interests are isolated, the better.— The only way to prevent smuggling and strife in a confederation of contiguous States, is to abolish custom-house lines from the interior, and declare free trade and free transit, (as in the United States,) collecting revenues and fostering home products by one custom-house line around the whole. This is the policy of the heavenly system—' that they *all* [not two and two] may be one.'

Note. 1.—The idea that amative magnetism can, by some miraculous agency peculiar to a state of perfection, be made to point only toward one object, (which is the hobby of some,) is very absurd. It is just as conceivable that a man should have an appetite for one apple but not for another equally good by the side of it, as that a man should have amative desire toward one woman, but not toward another equally attractive by the side of her. True, the will, backed by law and custom, may forbid the evolution of appetite into action in one case, and allow it in another ; but appetite itself is involuntary, and asks for that which is adapted to it, as indiscriminately in respect to women as to apples. If the sexual organs were so constructed that they could match only in pairs, we might believe that the affections which are connected with them, attract only in pairs. But as things are, it is quite as easy to believe that a man of integral nature and affections, should have no relish for the presence or the conversation of any woman but his wife, as that he should have no appetite for sexual interchange with any other. We say then, if the marriage fashion is to be continued, and amative appetite is to be suppressed in all directions except one, isolation is better than Association, since it makes less parade of forbidden fruit.

Note 2.—The only plausible method of avoiding the stumbling-blocks of the sexual question in Association, besides ours, is the method of the Shakers. Forbid sexual intercourse altogether, and you attain the same results, so far as shutting off the jealousies and strifes of exclusiveness is concerned, as will be attained by making sexual intercourse free. In this matter the Shakers show their shrewdness. But they sacrifice the vitality of society, in securing its peace.

Note 3.—Association, in o.der to be valuable, must be, not mere juxtaposition, but vital organization—not mere compaction of material, but community of life. Every member must be vitally organized, not only within itself, and into its nearest mate, but into the whole body, and must receive and distribute the common circulation. In a living body, (such as is the body of Christ,) the relation of the arm to the trunk is as intimate and vital as its relation to the hand, or as the relation of one part of it to another; and the relation of every member to the heart is as complete and essential, as the relation of each to its neighbor. A congeries of loose particles (i. e. individuals) cannot make a living body. No more can a congeries of loose double particles, (i. e. conjugal pairs.) The individuals and the pairs, as well as all larger combinations, must be knit together organically, and pervaded by one common life. Association of this kind will be to society what regeneration is to individuals—a resurrection from the dead. In the present order of isolation, society is dead. Association (genuine) will be properly named VITAL SOCIETY. Now as egotism in individuals obstructs the circulation of community life, (see Proposition viii.,) precisely so, exclusive conjugal love, which is only a double kind of egotism, obstructs community life. Vital society demands the surrender not only of property interests, and conjugal interests, but of life itself, or, if you please, personal identity, to the use of the whole. If this is the 'grave of liberty,' as the Fouricrists say, it is the grave of the liberty of selfishness, which has done mischief enough to deserve death—and it is the birth of the liberty of sociality. The whole gains more than individuals lose. In the place of dead society, we have vital society; and individuals have the liberty of harmony instead of the liberty of war.

PROPOSITION XXIII.—In vital society, strength will be increased, and the necessity of labor diminished, till all work will become sport, as it would have been in the original Eden state. See Gen. 2: 15, compare 3 : 17—19. Here we come to the field of the Fouricrists—the third link of the chain of evil. And here we shall doubtless ultimately avail ourselves of many of the economical and industrial discoveries of Fourier. But as the fundamental principle of our system differs entirely from that of Fourier, (our foundation being his superstructure, and *vice versa*,) and as every system necessarily has its own complement of external arrangements, conformed to its own genius, we will pursue our investigations for the present independently, and with special reference to our peculiar principles.—Labor is sport or drudgery,

according to the proportion between strength and the work
to be done. Work that overtasks a child, is easy to a man.
The amount of work remaining the same, if man's strength
were doubled, the result would be the same as if the amount
of work were diminished one half. To make labor sport, therefore, we must seek, first, increase of strength, and secondly,
diminution of work: or, (as in the former problem relating to
the curse on woman,) first, enlargement of income, and secondly, diminution of expenses. Vital society secures both of
these objects. It increases strength, by placing the individual
in a vital organization, which is in communication with the
source of life, and which distributes and circulates life with
the highest activity by the alternation of male and female.
In other words, as vital society is properly a resurrection-
state, so individuals in vital society will have the vigor of
resurrection. The amount of work to be done is correspondingly diminished. The staple necessaries of life are food,
raiment, shelter and fuel. The end of all these is the maintenance of vital heat. Liebeg says, and experience demonstrates, that food is fuel; and that the better men are clothed,
or the warmer their climate, the less food they need, especially
animal food. On the same principle we say, that the more
perfectly men are in communication with the source of vital
heat, and the more they are enveloped in the genial magnetism of social life, the less food, raiment, shelter, and fuel
they will need.

Note 1.—As society becomes vital and refined, drawing its best nour-
ishment from spiritual interchange, the grosser kinds of food, and especially animal food, will go out of use. The fruits of *trees* will become the
staple eatables. Gen. 2: 16. The largest part of the labor of the world
is now bestowed on the growth of anunal plants and animals. Cattle oc-
cupy more of the soil at present than men. The cultivation of trees will
be better sport than plowing, hoeing corn, digging potatoes, and waiting on
cows and pigs.

Note 2.—As society becomes compact and harmonious, its buildings
will be compact; and much labor now expended in accommodating egotism
and exclusiveness with isolated apartments, will be saved. The removal
of the partition between the sexes, will save many a partition to the car-

penter. In many other things, as well as buildings, love will save labor. Unity of hearts will prefer unity of accommodations as far as it is possible.

[*Note by the Compilers.*—The interior apartments of a house may be made by the arrangement of *curtain partitions*—the graceful folds of drapery, being substituted for lath-and-plaster walls. This combination of the primitive tent with the modern walled structure, allowing the circulation of air, heat and light from common sources through many rooms, and, at the same time, affording all desirable means of retirement to the occupants, has been tried at Oneida, and found to satisfy the highest claims of economy and taste.]

PROPOSITION XXIV.—In vital society, labor will become attractive. Loving companionship in labor, and especially the mingling of the sexes, makes labor attractive. The present division of labor between the sexes separates them entirely. The woman keeps house, and the man labors abroad. Men and women are married only after dark and during bed-time. Instead of this, in vital society men and women will mingle in both of their peculiar departments of work. It will be economically as well as spiritually profitable, to marry them indoors and out, by day as well as by night. When the partition between the sexes is taken away, and man ceases to make woman a propagative drudge, when love takes the place of shame, and fashion follows nature in dress and business, men and women will be able to mingle in all their employments, as boys and girls mingle in their sports; and then labor will be attractive.

Note 1.—The difference between the anatomical structures of men and women indicates the difference of their vocations. Men have their largest muscular developments in the upper part of the trunk, about the arms, and thus are best qualified for hand-labor. Women have their largest muscular developments in the lower part of the trunk, about the legs, and thus are best qualified for duties requiring locomotion. Girls outrun boys of the same age. The miraculous dancers are always females. How abusive then are the present arrangements, which confine women to the house! They are adapted by nature, even better than men, to out-door employments and sports—to running, leaping, &c.,—and yet they are excluded from every thing of this kind after childhood. They are not only shut up, but fettered. Gowns operate as shackles, and they are put on that sex which has most talent in the legs!

Note 2.—The present dress of women, besides being peculiarly inappropriate to the sex, is immodest. It makes the distinction between the sexes vastly more prominent and obtrusive than nature makes it. In a state of nature, the difference between a man and a woman could hardly be distinguished at a distance of five hundred yards; but as men and women dress, their sex is telegraphed as far as they can be seen.—Woman's dress is a standing lie. It proclaims that she is not a two-legged animal, but something like a churn, standing on castors! Such are the absurdities into which the false principle of shame and sexual isolation betray the world.

Note 3.—When the distinction of the sexes is reduced to the bounds of nature and decency, by the removal of the shame-partition, and woman becomes what she ought to be, a *female-man*, (like the Son in the Godhead,) a dress will be adopted that will be at the same time the most simple and the most beautiful; and it will be the same, or nearly the same, for both sexes. The dress of children—frock and pantalettes—is in good taste, i. e. taste not perverted by the dictates of shame; and it is well adapted to the free motion of both sexes. This, or something like it, will be the uniform of vital society.

[*Note by the Compilers.*—In consequence of these speculations on the subject of women's dress, in the summer of 1848 some of the leading women in the Association at Oneida took the liberty to dress themselves in short gowns or frocks, with pantalettes, (the fashion of dress common among children,) and the advantages of the change soon became so manifest, that others followed the example, till frocks and pantalettes became the prevailing fashion in the Association. Since that time this fashion has obtained considerable celebrity and success throughout the country under the name of 'Bloomerism.']

PROPOSITION XXV.—We can now see our way to victory over death. Reconciliation with God opens the way for the reconciliation of the sexes. Reconciliation of the sexes emancipates woman, and opens the way for vital society. Vital society increases strength, diminishes work, and makes labor attractive, thus removing the antecedents of death. First, we abolish sin; then shame; then the curse on woman of exhausting child-bearing; then the curse on man of exhausting labor; and so we arrive regularly at the tree of life, (as per Gen. 3.)

CHAPTER VII.

A concluding Caveat, that ought to be well noted by every Reader of the foregoing Argument.

PROPOSITION XXVI.—The will of God is done in heaven, and of course will be done in his kingdom on earth, not merely by general obedience to constitutional principles, but by specific obedience to the administration of his Spirit. The constitution of a nation is one thing, and the living administration of government is another. Ordinary theology directs attention chiefly, and almost exclusively, to the constitutional principles of God's government. (The same may be said of Fouricrism, and all schemes of reform based on the development of 'natural laws.') But as loyal subjects of God, we must give and call attention to his actual administration; i. e., to his will directly manifested by his Spirit and the agents of his Spirit, viz. his officers and representatives. We must look to God, not only for a Constitution, but for Presidential outlook and counsel; for a cabinet and corps of officers; for national aims and plans; for direction, not only in regard to principles to be carried out, but in regard to time and circumstance in carrying them out. In other words, the men who are called to usher in the kingdom of God, will be guided, not merely by theoretical truth, but by the Spirit of God, and specific manifestations of his will and policy, as were Abraham, Moses, David, Jesus Christ, Paul, &c. This will be called a fanatical principle, because it requires *bona fide* communication with the heavens, and displaces the sanctified maxim that the 'age of miracles and inspiration is past.' But it is clearly a Bible principle; and we must place it on high, above all others, as the palladium of conservatism in the introduction of the new social order, which we have proposed in the preceding Argument.

Note 1.—The principles of sexual morality which have been presented, are called incendiary and dangerous; and they are incendiary and dangerous, as fire, steam, gun-powder, &c. are, in unfit hands. We shall endeavor (as we have done) to keep them out of unfit hands: and we hereby notify all, that we neither license or encourage any one to attempt the practice of these incendiary theories, without clear directions from the government in the heavens. No movement in these matters can be made safely, in the way of imitation, or on the mere ground of acquaintance with the theory of the new order of things. Other qualifications besides theoretical knowledge, are requisite for the construction and handling of a locomotive; and much more for the management of such tremendous machinery as that of vital society. Let no man attempt the work, without the charter and manifest patronage of the general government. Of course we cannot prevent children from playing with fire, but we forewarn them that they will burn their fingers.

Note 2.—The first qualification for office in the kingdom of God, and especially for employment in the critical operations of the revolution in sexual matters, manifestly is true spirituality, securing inspiration; and true spirituality cannot be attained without true holiness, i. e. self-crucifixion, and the love-devotion described by Paul in 1 Cor. 13: 4—7. The government in heaven will not employ self-seekers; and whoever meddles with the affairs of the inner sanctuary without being employed by the government, will plunge himself into consuming fire. Thus official distinctions and love-rewards, in the kingdom of God, will be bounties on true spirituality and holiness. If a man desires place and emolument, let him first show that he holds ' the mystery of faith in a pure conscience.'— 1 Tim. 3: 9.

PART III.

DOCTRINAL FOUNDATIONS.

[Most of the following articles are selections from *The Circular*, and as they were not written consecutively, or with a view to the present combination, the reader must expect to find in them some repetition and informality; but with due attention he will get from them a fair view of the GOSPEL, as understood by Bible Communists, in its bearings on social questions and human institutions.]

CRITICISM OF CHRISTENDOM.

THE apostasy of the United States from their original principles in respect to Slavery, affords precisely the illustration that is needed, to set forth the backsliding of Christendom, from the standard of original Christianity. Let us glance at the facts in the case of the nation, and then extend the parallel to the history of the Christian world.

The Revolutionary fathers of this government, it is admitted, were bent on establishing Republicanism in this country. The equality of mankind—liberty for all—was their motto, and the idea which they fought for. They knew no other.—They put forth in all their words and acts the broad, universal principles of freedom, without limit, proviso, or qualification, manifestly intending that equality should rule throughout the country. But Slavery, as an institution, was then in existence, and they found it necessary, for the time being, to tolerate it as a fact, though they ignored it as a principle.—As an established relation, it required some prudential lenity, and some time and preparation wisely to dispose of it. The nation conceded this necessary toleration, but only on terms of

5

temporary expediency—only with a view to the necessary practical transition which should rid the country of it altogether. The slave-trade was put in the way to be abolished, and all the measures and arguments of the government were directed towards the extinction of the institution. They made no defence of Slavery, but intended to bring it to an end as fast as they could. The Northern States proceeded in good faith to abolish it within their limits; and all parties were agreed that the Declaration of Independence was the firm, eternal standard of principle, to which all our institutions must ultimately conform.

But what is the present position of the country? The doctrine now is, that Slavery is a good thing—the corner-stone of our Republican edifice. This is the position of the whole South, and is acquiesced in, it is said, by a large majority of the nation. They tell us that Slavery is entirely justifiable —that they intend to keep it, have no notion of ever abolishing it, and will resent any interference with it. Here is a radical change. Originally, the Declaration of Independence, which stated things as they *ought to be,* was considered the standard toward which things as they are should tend; now the doctrine is reversed, and *things as they are,* are the standard to which all the theories and efforts of the country must conform.

Turning now to the case of Christianity, we find that precisely a similar process of apostasy and perversion has taken place. Christendom has treated the original gospel in the same way that the people of the United States have treated the Declaration of Independence; i. e., advantage has been taken of its prudential, transitionary toleration of existing evils, to exalt them into corner-stones; and thus its main design has been subverted, and its foundation-principles dishonored.

Christianity came, setting forth broad, absolute principles, which, like the Declaration of Independence were intended as the foundation of a government—were to form the Constitution of the Kingdom of Heaven. But it came into a world covered with sin and the devil's works, and as in the case of the founders of the Republic in their dealings with Slavery, it had to accommodate itself, for the time being, to the evil which it found, and provide for a transition. It stated boldly and clearly the principles of things as they ought to be, and yet was considerate and gentle towards things as they were. Christ and the apostles were men of moderation and prudence. Their absolute principles, as well as their transitionary ones, required that they should abstain from rash and violent attempts at outward change. But they held themselves and the world firmly to the *standard* which the gospel brought, and contemplated the entire abolition of the devil's works, just as soon as possible. They were looking for and hasting unto the day when the old heavens and earth would pass away, together with all the policy and experience of the transition period.

But what is the position of professed followers of Christ now? Evidently the same kind of change has passed upon Christendom, that has happened in this country with reference to Slavery. The Christian world has finally settled itself into the attitude of working for and defending that which was only a transitionary policy of the apostles, as being the true and permanent Constitution. It has taken advantage of the temporary accommodation which the gospel manifested toward various evils, to set them up on high as sacred institutions. We will notice a few of the instances in which this thing has been done.

In the first place, according to the Constitution of Christianity, *sin was to be abolished* in this world. This is evident from the fact that Christ, the founder of the dispensation, was without sin. He came to introduce into the world the Constitution of the kingdom of heaven ; and as there is no sin there, his mission necessarily involved the abolition of it here. We have the plainest possible proof in all the declarations of the New Testament, that Christianity contemplated the entire removal of sin, as in the passages—'For this pur-

pose the Son of God was manifested, that he might destroy
the works of the devil'—'He that is born of God doth not
commit sin,' 'He that commiteth sin is of the devil,' &c.

With such a clear constitutional tendency and such an end
in view, the gospel came into a world full of sin, under complete possession, as it were, of the devil.   In these circumstances the moderation of Christ would dictate the favorable
and indulgent application of its principles to those who were
involved in existing evil, so as not to stumble and destroy
those whom he could reach and save.   He did not let loose
immediate and condemning judgment upon all sinners, but
left room for those who were ignorant and out of the way, to
come to a more perfect knowledge of him.   In the benevolence of his accommodation to a transitional state of things, he
even tolerated more or less imperfection in the church.   But
observe, *this was incidental policy, and not the permanent
constitutional truth which he came to establish.*   The great
unqualified Principles of Christianity—'He that committeth
sin is of the devil—He that is born of God doth not commit
sin'—were left in full force, and every thing was expected to
conform to this standard.

But what is the state of public opinion and Christian belief
on this point now ?   Why, that sin cannot be abolished, and
never is to be abolished in this world.   It is inherent, they
say, in the constitution of man : a necessary evil, that we
cannot do without.   Thus like Slavery, it has come to be regarded as a permanent institution ; and the great declarations of the gospel on the subject of perfect holiness, have fallen like the Declaration of Independence into mere rhetorical
flourishes, to be repeated for popular effect, in glorifying the
existing state of things.

A second point in the great perversion of Christendom
which we will notice, is in relation to Marriage.   We observe,
in the first place, that Jesus Christ and Paul, the two
leaders of Christianity, did not marry.   Christ said also, that
in the kingdom of heaven they neither marry nor are given

in marriage; and then he proceeded to exhort men not to lay up treasures on earth, but to lay up for themselves treasures in heaven. All his teachings tended to urge men into a state in which marriage should pass away ; and it was expected that in the final triumph of his kingdom and principles on the earth, that institution would be swallowed up in universal unity. In accordance with this view, Paul, though he would put the church under no constraint of conscience, yet plainly expressed his opinion that it was best for them not to marry. In this case, as in the others which we have noticed, there was an interval of transition to be provided for, a margin of discretionary, prudential management, between the existing state of things, which was passing away, and the full operation of those constitutional principles which were acknowledged in the church. Paul's doctrine on marriage was explicitly adapted to this transition interval. It exhibits the prudence of a man who, in getting out of the world, seeks to avoid a violent and destructive process. While his eye was continually on the heavenly state, toward which he and the church were tending, he also saw things as they were, and accommodated his doctrine with consummate skill, to the necessities then present. He both approved and disapproved of marriage. As a constitutionalist, he was opposed to it, and knew that it was passing away : as an administrator, and expedientist, he considered it honorable, and condemned those who forbade it. This is the only view which can reconcile the seeming contradictions of his attitude on this subject.

But the world, leaving entirely the standard of absolute principle which Paul and Christ inculcated, have settled down on their incidental transitionary policy, and have made marriage, as they have sin, a permanent, immovable institution. Both of these things were *passing away* in the Primitive church, and their toleration in the gospel was founded entirely on that idea. Now, that which was bare toleration and expediency, is turned round and made the substance of the gospel itself. Sin is incorporated into the perpetual foun-

dations of the church: and marriage is said to be the corner-
stone of society, and even of Christianity itself.

But this brings us to another point in the examination—
the position of Christendom on the subject of *human governments.* It is evident that Christ came to establish the kingdom of heaven on earth, and of course to abolish human governments. He was rightfully king of the world, and all his
teachings showed that he was preparing to assert that supremacy. The single passage, 'My kingdom is not of this world,'
in consequence of an obscure translation is sometimes made to
look like a disclaimer of earthly sovereignty; but it is not one.
Christ's idea was not that his kingdom is not to come *upon*
this world and supersede all other governments, but simply
that it did not *originate* in this world, and is not supported
and propagated by carnal weapons; 'else,' says he, ' would
my servants fight: but now is my kingdom not *from
hence.*' He did proceed in the course of forty years to assert
his sovereignty over the nations. In the case of the Jewish nation, there was a civil government that was allowed and
prospered by God for a long time, and doubtless it was the
best thing for the world during its continuance; but it
was utterly annihilated at the destruction of Jerusalem.—
Christ dashed it in pieces at his Second Coming. And the
promise was that his kingdom should finally break in pieces
and consume all other kingdoms, and stand forever. During
the intermediate transition, the church, as usual, were counselled to moderation and obedience; but there can be no
doubt that his design was to come into the world and take
the place of all other governments. What is the position of
Christianity now in this respect? The answer is, the Church
and State are separated, and the State is put over the Church
in nearly the whole civilized world; and human government is
held up as a perpetual and sacred ordinance, never to be dis-
turbed. On this point again, modern Christendom has entirely abandoned the absolute principles which declare how
things ought to be, and planted itself on transition principles.

Finally, the pioneers of Christianity proclaimed their intention of abolishing *Death;* and they expected this would be done, just as confidently as our forefathers expected the abolition of Slavery. It was a constitutional principle with them. But how does the world now feel about it ? Men generally do not entertain the first idea of the thing. Death is one of their permanent institutions, baptized and sanctified, and never to be destroyed.

The republican compact of our forefathers in this country, though it refrained from putting an end to Slavery at once, yet contemplated its abolition, at a future time ; and the Abolitionists, believing that that time has now come, feel justified in making a direct attack. So there was contemplated in the Constitution of Christianity, the abolition not only of Slavery, but of all kindred institutions; and it is right for men now to inquire whether the time for the accomplishment of its provisions has not come. It is time for Christians to inquire *what* the gospel was designed to abolish, and to take their stand there. The scope of its intention in this respect, must be judged by a consideration of the fact that Christ, its author, was a man without sin, who came professedly to introduce heaven upon earth. Sin was previously the central principle to which all the institutions and governments of the world were conformed. Christ's appearing ' to make an end of sin,' therefore, involved the ultimate subversion of the entire fashion of this world.

CONSTITUTIONAL CHRISTIANITY.

WE get the simplest and clearest idea of the gospel as a radical, organizing force, or in other words, of *Constitutional Christianity*, by fixing our attention on the central fact in its history—*the death and resurrection of Christ.* This was evidently *the* fact of absorbing interest with Paul and the Primitive church; and there can be no mistake in saying that it involves, in one way or another, the whole mystery of salvation.

To state in the simplest way, the circumstances of the event:—A man who had lived in this world for an appointed time, and gathered about him a company of disciples, *died;* and in a short time afterwards *arose from the dead,* and reäppeared to his disciples. And, (tracing the matter into its consequences,) this resurrection-man—this *posthumous* leader, if we may so call him, became *the head of a church;* and became so by the distribution of a spiritual influence, (commencing mainly, from the day of Pentecost,) which assimilated those that believed on him to himself, in such a manner that it was proper to call the church his *body.* So much is plain and indisputable.

But let us dwell on this latter fact a little. The Primitive church was evidently a body of men and women who were joined to Christ, or as Paul expresses it, were 'baptized into him ;' and by this spiritual baptism having, as it were, dropped their own lives and taken his, they were called his body. But Christ, their head and leader, was a posthumous, resurrection-man. And because they were thus vitally identified with him as his body, the state into which he had come by dying and rising from the dead passed down also upon them; so that they could claim to be crucified with him, and to be risen with him ; it was with them as with him. As he was a posthumous being, who had died and risen again, so that church was a posthumous church, claiming the same death and resurrection, and proving itself to be not of this world by the same logic that proved its head to be not of this world. This, as we understand it, is the palpable truth on the face of the whole New Testament, and therefore the germ and center of Constitutional Christianity.

The annunciation of this idea, however, immediately impels the mind forward to a consideration of its consequences; and we cannot but see at once that, simple as it is, a tremendous revolution is involved in it. The assumption of a posthumous state and position in this world, on the ground of union with a posthumous being who became the head of the church, and who made the church his body, and so identified himself with men that they could say they were dead and risen with him,—such an assumption, though necessarily deduced from the facts in the case, was yet the most revolutionary step that men could take. The establishment of such a Constitution for Christianity involved ultimate consequences of the profoundest character.

That we may not seem to be making assertions without proof, we will introduce here, specimens of Paul's language to four of the Primitive churches, in which a strong light is thrown upon this radical principle of Christianity, and the consequences which the apostles drew from it. In the following, he is urging the Romans to apprehend the privilege of the posthumous state to which they were translated by fellowship with the death and resurrection of Christ, in respect to *freedom from sin.*

"How shall we that are dead to sin, live any longer therein? Know ye not, that so many of us as were baptized into Jesus Christ, were baptized into his death? Therefore, we are buried with him by baptism into death: that like as Christ was raised up from the dead by the glory of the Father, even so we also should walk in newness of life. For if we have been planted together in the likeness of his death, we shall be also in the likeness of his resurrection : knowing this, that our old man is crucified with him, that the body of sin might be destroyed, that henceforth we should not serve sin. For he that is dead is freed from sin. Now if we be dead with Christ, we believe that we shall also live with him; knowing that Christ being raised from the dead, dieth no more: death hath no more dominion over him. For in that he died, he died unto sin once: but in that he liveth, he liveth unto God. Likewise, reckon ye also yourselves to be dead indeed unto sin, but alive unto God through Jesus Christ our Lord." Rom. 6: 2—11.

In another place, he reminds them of their emancipation from the dominion of the *law,* by the fact of their death and transfer to another world:

"Know ye not, brethren, (for I speak to them that know the law,) how that the law hath dominion over a man as long as he liveth? For the woman which hath a husband is bound by the law to her husband so long as he liveth: but if the husband be dead, she is loosed from the law of her husband. So then if, while her husband liveth, she be married to another man, she shall be called an adulteress : but if her husband be dead, she is free from that law ; so that she is no adulteress though she be married to another man. Wherefore, my brethren, ye also are become dead to the law by the body of Christ; that ye should be married to another, even to him who is raised from the dead, that we should bring forth fruit unto God. For when we were in the flesh, the motions of sins, which were by the law, did work in our members to bring forth fruit unto death. But now we are delivered from the law, that being dead wherein we were held; that we should serve in newness of spirit, and not in the oldness of the letter." 7: 1—6.

The same sentiment is again repeated in Galatians :

"For I through the law am dead to the law, that I might live unto God. I am crucified with Christ: nevertheless I live; yet not I, but Christ liveth in me; and the life which I now live in the flesh I live by the faith of the Son of God, who loved me, and gave himself for me." Gal. 2: 19, 20.

In another place he states the principle broadly, that in the death of Christ all died ; and makes it the ground for disavowing all those external connections which obtain in the world :

"The love of Christ constraineth us ; because we thus judge, that if one died for all, then all died ; [Greek ;] and that he died for all, that they which live should not henceforth live unto themselves, but unto him which died for them and rose again. Wherefore henceforth know we no man after the flesh; yea, though we have known Christ after the flesh, yet now henceforth know we him no more. Therefore, if any man be in Christ, he is a new creature; old things are passed away; behold, all things are become new." 2 Cor. 5: 14—17.

For the same admitted reason, he takes occasion to reprove the Colossians, (2: 20—23,) for their observance of legal ordinances—Sabbaths, holy days, &c. :

"Wherefore (says he) if ye be DEAD with Christ from the rudiments of the world, why, as though living in the world, are ye subject to ordinances, (touch not, taste not, handle not ; which all are to perish with the using;) after the commandments and doctrines ot men ? . . . .

"If ye then be risen with Christ, (he continues,) seek those things which are above, where Christ sitteth on the right hand of God. Set your affection on things above, and not on things on the earth. For YE ARE DEAD, and your life is hid with Christ in God. When Christ, who is our life, shall appear, then shall ye also appear with him in glory."

The passages we have cited speak for themselves, and show plainly that the intent of the gospel was, and is, to take people out of this world into a state beyond death, in which the believer is spiritually with Christ in the resurrection, and hence is free from sin and law, and all the temporary relations of the mortal state. In other words, Christ stands in the place of death to those who receive him, having all the prerogatives of death, and just as effectually taking them out of the world with all its claims and connections, as though they went through the process of separation from the body in the old way. This is the superiority of the gospel, the grace that comes by Christ, which the prophets and patriarchs of previous dispensations never knew. This is the meaning, faintly shadowed, of Paul's great doctrine of '*Christ crucified*,' which unto the Jews was a stumbling-block, and unto the Greeks foolishness; 'but unto them which are called, both Jews and Greeks, Christ the power of God, and the wisdom of God.'

It is in order now to inquire what was the practical operation of this tremendous doctrine in the Primitive church. How far did its legitimate consequences take effect in their outward relations? We may see at a glance, that it produced among them some very important revolutionary consequen-

ces in relation to *law*. It is a matter of history that
the Primitive church did claim on the ground of their
identity with Christ's death and resurrection, emancipation from the ceremonies of the Jewish law. This
fact is plain on the face of the New Testament ; and it
will be remembered, that at that time, in that age and
country, the abrogation of circumcision, and all the sacred
institutions of the Mosaic economy, was a very serious matter. It was accounted seditious and revolutionary in the
highest degree ; and roused all the conservatism of the Jews
on the one hand, and required all the heroism of the martyr-
spirit in the church on the other. So far, at least, the church
went, in following out the great constitutional principle of
Christianity, that in the death and resurrection of Christ,
the believer is carried out of this world, and into the post-
mortal state, where Christ is.

Still it is plain in the New Testament history, that
the inevitable consequences of that primary idea were not *all*
developed in the Primitive church. The *subversive* operation
of it in reference to the institutions of this world was limited
—as can easily be seen and shown—and it was limited, recollect, in reference to institutions that are *now* being attacked.
The Primitive church did not attack *slavery* at all; and
yet probably most persons believe that the destruction of slavery was somewhere concealed in the Constitution of Christianity and in the doctrines of the Primitive church. But
leaving slavery, the only civil and religious institutions which
Christianity directly attacked at that time were those immediately connected with the Mosaic economy: institutions however, which were as sacred to the Jew, as slavery is to the
South, or as marriage is to mankind in general. These it
subverted, but left the Gentile world mainly undisturbed.

It is natural then to inquire how and why it was that such
a revolutionary central principle as we have stated—the professed standing of the church in a posthumous state—could
be consistent with the conservatism which we see in its his-

tory in regard to slavery and other such institutions. The Primitive church manifestly did stand in a conservative attitude towards even vicious institutions; there was manifestly a compromise between the absolute principle on which it was founded, and its actual course toward existing things. Let us discover, if we can, the broad principle by which this is to be interpreted.

Our view is, that the apostles did not choose to spend their force or to turn the attention of men on any of the minor, secondary elements and institutions of the world ; and hence they chose not to place themselves in direct quarrel with slavery, or with civil governments, any further than it was necessary to develop the *principle* of freedom ; and *that* they did in their warfare with the Jewish ritual. Their wisdom and their actual course was, first of all, to make an end of *sin ;* and accordingly we find that there is the spot where they first brought to bear this resurrection-lever—on sin, as being the center of all selfish institutions; and on the clear economical principle that if you destroy the *root* of a thing, all its branches will die. Of all the recognized institutions of the *present* world, the only one that was directly attacked by the power of Christ's resurrection, in the times of the Primitive church, was *sin.* The sixth chapter of Romans tells the story—it was the ' body of sin' that was to be destroyed. And it was because they struck at the root, that they neglected the branches.

A person who does not understand this principle, will wonder why the apostles did not let loose their artillery of denunciation against slavery; but they evidently did not, and with the very good reason that they knew if they could destroy sin, that all such institutions as slavery, which are the expressions of sin, would come to an end of themselves. And there is no doubt that in attacking sin, or in other words, selfishness, they expected in process of time, that all institutions originating in selfishness, or expressing selfishness, and all institutions made for the purpose of controlling, rectifying, and repressing selfishness, would come to an end. It should be noticed that many of those institutions that on the one hand, express selfishness, are on the other hand fitted to be its regulators, and the Primitive church would not allow themselves to stand as destructives, removing the *safeguards* of society, before they had destroyed selfishness, which is the *danger* of society. If they had turned aside to attack institutions which curb and punish sin, it would have been really a destructive operation ; but on the other hand, confining their attacks to the abolition of selfishness, they knew perfectly well that all institutions which are in any way connected with it, would fall to ruin with the success of their enterprise.

Such was their function in relation to slavery. They certainly did not say any thing against it by itself ; on the contrary they discountenanced the disturbance of that relation so long as the sources of it remained; they were opposed to slaves running away, &c. But it is equally certain that they brought to bear on slavery a sure power of ultimate destruction, by their attacks on its source, which is selfishness.

But while we thus perceive and concede that the resurrection principle was confined in its operations mainly to the source of evil in the heart, leaving externals for the time being to go on as usual, we must not forget the central fact that a *posthumous man was the head of the church*, and that its foundation principle derived from this fact, was a *growing, expansive* thing, which must necessarily advance in its conquests, and finally break up every thing connected with sin, or foreign to the resurrection. It was surely a revolutionary gospel, that began from the resurrection of Christ. A *vortex* was then formed, of death to sin and selfishness, and all evil— a resurrection-vortex, around which all men and institutions from that time began to circle, and into which they must all sooner or later plunge. And as all men and institutions must go into that vortex, whatsoever does not belong to the resurrection man, must there *go down*.

Now let us go forward and try the bearing of this view of

the gospel of Christ upon the institutions of the present time. All will admit probably the view we have taken of the operation of Christianity in respect to slavery—that though it did not immediately and directly attack that institution, yet it attacked its source, and that now slavery itself is about plunging into the vortex which the gospel formed, and will be destroyed by it. So much will be readily seen and conceded. But here we have to notice that there is a curious linking together in the New Testament, of slavery and marriage. The two subjects are uniformly found in connection, and there is a remarkable resemblance in the apostolic treatment of them. You find in the epistle to the Ephesians, 'Wives, submit yourselves unto your own husbands—Husbands, love your wives ;' and right after that, 'Servants, be obedient to your masters,' &c. Go into Colossians, and you find the same thing—marriage and slavery in close connection, and the same kind of advice administered for both. Take up the first epistle to the Corinthians, at the chapter devoted to the subject of marriage, and you will find a significant allusion to slavery, showing that the two occupied the same platform in the apostle's mind. Speaking of marriage, he says, 'Art thou bound unto a wife ? seek not to be loosed. Art thou loosed from a wife ? seek not a wife.' Then in the same connection : 'Art thou called being a servant [slave] ? care not for it ; but if thou mayest have thy liberty, use it rather.' Go even to that text which is so conspicuous with the particular friends of marriage—'Marriage is honorable in all'—and you will find in the verse next before it, 'Remember them that are in bonds, as bound with them.' Paul coupled the two institutions of slavery and marriage together, and treated them alike, with this difference : that he no where came out with a point-blank argument against slavery, as he did against marriage. There is one chapter in his epistles, (1 Cor. 7,) which is devoted to general advice against marriage. Christ also, in his celebrated remark about the resurrection, omits to notice slavery, but affirms that there is no marriage there. We judge from these signs, that if they had felt themselves called to go beyond attacking sin and the Mosaic institutions, in the place of attacking slavery first, they would have attacked marriage.

It may be said that the apostles not only abstained from attacking marriage in a subversive way, but that they severely reprimanded any violation of the law of marriage, as fornication, adultery, &c. That is certainly true. These offenses bore the same relation to marriage, precisely, that the running away and disobedience of the slaves bear to slavery ; and on the same principle that they reprobated a violation of marriage, they reprobated the disobedience of slaves. Paul sent back Onesimus. We are disposed to think, indeed, from the attitude which they assumed in reference to the mode of attacking vicious institutions, that they would not have resisted even the present Fugitive Slave Law. Their general principle was that of leaving the institutions of the world to pass away by the ultimate effect of the abolition of sin. In view of the existing marriage code, fornication and adultery were in their view like violent attempts to escape from slavery, or like smuggling, involving the breaking of law, and the mischiefs of social disorder. The assertion of liberty, either social or civil, would have been equivalent then to disorganization, and hence it was manifestly untimely and uninspired, and was therefore uniformly opposed.

We have brought to view in a fair and indisputable manner, the Constitution of Christianity, by which the church of believers assumed the condition of their crucified and risen Head, and the practical policy of the Primitive church, under that Constitution.

The question how we shall follow in their footsteps in the application of that Constitution to the present time, is a somewhat complicated problem ; and a conscientious man will search long and seriously for some clue by which he may be sure that he is following out the principles which they stood upon. We will not undertake in this article to show

how these principles are to be applied by us as followers of them at the present time. But thus much we do say: that as loyal believers with them in the gospel of Christ, and re-ceivers of their understanding of the Constitution of Chris-tianity, we are bound now and at all times, in all places and forever, to hold forth the constitutional principles which have been stated. We are bound to accept a posthumous state as the Constitution of Christianity. We are bound to sweep the field of all obstructions to a clear view of that fact; and if any institutions now rise up and deny God's right to have a posthumous church in this world, then we shall have to face them, and demand in the name of the living God, the rights of Christianity in this respect.

That is the broad ground we stand upon. The original faith of 'Christ crucified' must not only be revived, but it must have the liberty of expansion and growth; and the things that belong to this world must make room for it. The original vortex of Christianity must at all hazards be re-opened, and all earthly institutions, circling around it, must take their chance. If they belong to the *heavenly* state, they will survive; and if they do not belong to the heavenly state, they will go down.

We need not stop to look at the consequences of this posi-tion; we are perfectly safe in adopting Paul's motto, and there need be no question as to what that was. ' I am cru-cified with Christ,'—'I am determined not to know any-thing among you, save Jesus Christ and him crucified,' &c. This was Paul's gospel, and that of the Primitive church. Their grand thought was not the abolition of this or that specific evil, but the great antecedent idea, that by the death of Christ they were dead and risen with him. By joining and becoming united to a resurection-man, they also were taken out of this world with him. This is *Constitutional Chris-tianity ;* and we are sure it will ultimately sweep all before it. There is no answer to it : it is safe, and the power and inspiration of God will go with it.

6

THE BIBLE ON MARRIAGE.

WE avow ourselves strictly and entirely Bible men—disciples of the New Testament, of Christ and of Paul, in relation to the subject of marriage. We do not on the one hand turn aside as some do, to independent philosophical speculation ; nor do we appeal with others to the authority of a new revelation. We adhere only to the Bible, and feel bound in every respect to abide by the judgment of those who have gone before us in the gospel. We sincerely believe in the inspiration of the New Testament teachers, and that their views, sooner or later, will be found to be eternal truth, proceeding from God. All that we want is, to know precisely *what they did teach* in relation to marriage,—to have a thorough understanding of them, and not misrepresent their views to ourselves or others.

So much as this is perfectly clear : that they were not in favor of *freedom of divorce*, as a means of mitigating the difficulties connected with marriage. There cannot be any mistake about the fact that Christ, instead of being in favor of freedom of divorce, as it had existed under the Mosaic dispensation, restored the law to its simplicity and rigor, allowing no divorce except in cases of adultery. (Mark 10.) And Paul stood substantially on the same ground ; that is, he forbade believers for any cause to sunder the external marriage tie. (1 Cor. 7.) It is true he supposed the case of separation brought about by the departure of an unbelieving partner, and said that the other was not in bondage in such cases.— Whether this in his mind amounted to the privilege of divorce and marrying again, we cannot perhaps determine ; but at all events, it was his will that the whole movement and responsibility of separation should be laid on the unbeliever. He did not allow *the gospel* to introduce separation between husband and wife, or to relax at all the marriage code.

The Bible view of divorce may be illustrated thus: Suppose a commercial system which brings people into a general condition of debt, one to another. Now one way to mitigate this fact and release people from such a state of things, would be by enacting a general Bankrupt law, which would make an end of all obligations by legal repudiation. The Bankrupt law operates to release a man from his promises; and this is just the nature of any legal increase of freedom of divorce.— Christ and Paul, however, were clearly opposed to any Bankrupt law in relation to marriage, as being a mode of discharge not contemplated in the original contract, and as dishonestly rescinding unlimited obligations.

Sympathizing with them in this respect, we as Bible Communists are on entirely different ground from that of the infidels and Owenites of twenty years ago; and from that of James and nearly all of those who are now seeking to bring about a revolution in regard to marriage. We will loyally abide by the view of Christ and of Paul on that subject. If there is to be any alleviation of the miseries of marriage, it is not to come by freedom of divorce.

Again, we are clear that the teachings of the New Testament were sufficiently distinct against *polygamy*. We do not recollect any thing very positive and decisive on this point that can be quoted; but there is a strong intimation of Paul's opinion in the passage where he says, ' a bishop must be the husband of one wife.' (1 Tim. 3: 2.)

We do not think it is fair at all to infer any thing against polygamy from the saying that 'what God hath joined together men must not put asunder'—the original doctrine of the inviolability of contracts on which Christ insisted in regard to marriage—because it is not a matter of course that a man shall abandon his first wife by taking a second. No such thing did happen, under the polygamic economy of the patriarchs; on the contrary it was well understood that the contract with the first wife could be fulfilled consistently with taking a second. Christ in that saying is pointing his artillery against putting away. If polygamy were understood to be a nullification of any previous marriage, then that saying would operate against it. But there is no intimation of any such thing in the New Testament, and hence the objection to polygamy must be placed on other grounds.

We have seen in the passage referring to bishops, an indication of Paul's preference of monogamy over polygamy.— But it must likewise be noticed in this connection that he preferred agamy, or having no wives, to monogamy. His disapprobation of polygamy is not necessarily to be taken as in favor of monogamy. On the contrary his objection was against marriage altogether, as causing trouble in the flesh, and as being a distraction to believers. (1 Cor. 7: 28, &c.) His objection to marriage in general is primarily an objection to monogamy ; and of course much more to polygamy, as being a still worse distraction.

Here we may dwell for a moment on the identity in principle of monogamy with polygamy. And it will then be seen, that in following Christ we are further from the position of polygamists than ordinary society. It is plain that the fundamental principle of monogamy and polygamy is the same ; to wit, the ownership of woman by man. The monogamist claims one woman as his wife—the polygamists, two or a dozen; but the essential thing, the bond of relationship constituting marriage, in both cases is the same, namely, a claim of ownership.

The similarity and the difference between monogamy and polygamy, may be illustrated thus : Suppose slavery to be introduced into Pennsylvania, but limited by law, so that no man can own more than *one* slave. That might be taken to represent monogamy, or the single wife system. In another State suppose men are allowed to own any number they please. That corresponds to polygamy. Now what would be the difference between these two States, in respect to slavery ? There

would be a difference in the details, and external limitations of
the system, but identity in principle. The State· that allowed a man to have but one slave, would be on the same
general basis of principle with the State that allowed him to
have a hundred. Such, we conceive, is the relation ·between
monogamy and polygamy; and as we understand the New
Testament, the state which Jesus Christ and Paul were in
favor of was neither, but a state of entire freedom from both.

Monogamy allows a man but one wife; polygamy allows a
plurality. In choosing between them Paul naturally prefers
that which comes nearest to the resurrection-standard, and says
virtually, ' If you marry at all, it is best to have but one wife;
but it is better still not to have any.' He set this example
himself, and evidently intended to encourage the entire abolition of marriage, which is the furthest possible distance from
polygamy—further from polygamy than monogamy.

We find ourselves, then, as followers of the New Testament,
standing far apart from those who wish to ameliorate the miseries of marriage by a bankrupt law, i. e., a law for free divorce:
and far apart from polygamists, who propose to give a liberty
of multiplying wives; that is, to expand the principle of monogamy, which is ownership. The Bible position is entirely
different from either of these.

And now we must try to ascertain more definitely the precise position of Paul and Christ on the subject of marriage.
It is plain that the absolute constitutional principle in which
they stood personally, toward which they were leading the
church, and which they expected would expand itself, and oc-
cupy the field which is now occupied by monogamy, polygamy,
&c., is declared in that saying of Christ, '*In the resurrection
they neither marry nor are given in marriage.*' They were
pressing on the church the importance of living in heaven—
becoming in reality citizens of heaven. ' If ye then be risen
with Christ, seek those things which are above.' ' Lay not
up for yourselves treasures upon earth, where moth and rust
do corrupt; but lay up for yourselves treasures in heaven,'

&c.; i. e., 'Do not seek temporary fellowships, like marriage, &c., but lay up for yourselves eternal connections.' And that we may be sure that they were bent on introducing the heavenly state of things into this world, Christ put that prayer into his disciples' mouths,—' Thy kingdom come, thy will be done ON EARTH AS IT IS DONE IN HEAVEN.'

We have then their position defined, negatively at least, with perfect certainty—a position not in favor of divorce, not in favor of polygamy, and finally, not in favor of marriage itself; but tending to abolish it altogether. Such a view of their position, and such alone, will reconcile their various sayings and doings on the subject.

There is some seeming inconsistency in the idea of their being opposed to divorce and to marriage too. It may be said, "If marriage is to be abolished, that of course *is* divorce; and if they were in favor of the one, they must have been of the other." Inconsistency or not, we reply, these two things are there—on the one hand, prohibition of freedom of divorce, and on the other, a pressure against marriage altogether; and we must reconcile them as best we can.

In explanation of the difficulty we have to rise a little into what may be called a *spiritualizing* view of things : but to us it is none the less satisfactory, since it is surely the Christian view.

The doctrine that *death* is the legitimate end of the contract of marriage, is distinctly conceded by all. ' A woman is bound by the law to her husband as long as he liveth; but if the husband be dead she is loosed from the law of her husband.' Paul and Christ were certainly not in favor of divorce by any other power than that of death. They adhered to the principle of marriage *for life* without any essential exceptions. *But they found a way to introduce what may be called a posthumous state into this world, by the application of the death of Christ.* Their doctrine, as was shown fully in a previous article, was, that by believing in Christ we are crucified with him. ' If one died for all, then all died.' It may be said that the apostle did not intend to apply the death here spoken of to marriage. We reply, he certainly did apply it as a release from other worldly ordinances. The whole Jewish law was over the church, and it was like the law of marriage, in that it was over them *for life;* and the only outlet from its ordinances, to the conscientious Jew, was by death.—— Yet Paul every where proclaimed release from them, by union with the death of Christ. Though he did not carry the principle out in reference to marriage, it is perfectly clear that the same logic that would make an end of any part of the Jewish law, would make an end of marriage. If that is a substantial principle of the gospel, (and it seems to us to be the very *center* of it,) then we can see how they could oppose divorce and yet favor the abolition of marriage, in view of the *posthumous* state that was to come in this world by virtue of the death and resurrection of Christ. They certainly contemplated that posthumous state as their landing place, and were pressing towards it; and in view of entering into it as fast as possible, they discouraged marriage; preferring not to encumber themselves with transitory ties, but seeking rather with their whole hearts the resurrection-state.

And here we will remark again, that this doctrine of the believer's death and resurrection by union with Christ, however foolish it may seem now, was in the Primitive church the very core of the gospel. They realized the fact that they were past death, and so were delivered from sin and legality, by the cross of Christ. This is the meaning of those frequent declarations of Paul, ' I am crucified with Christ'—'I am determined not to glory, save in the cross of Christ, whereby I am crucified to the world, and the world to me,' &c. This doctrine and belief had a tremendous practical bearing upon their character and position; and it is the grand apostasy of Christendom, that it has since lost sight of it. The cross of Christ, putting men through death and into a posthumous state, is certainly the spiritual truth which must be restored to the throne of Christianity.

This principle, as we have said, was not carried through into all its bearings on marriage; but Paul *did carry it out so far as to demand that the heart should assume the eternal, heavenly state ;* for he says, ' Let them that have wives be as though they had none.' So that in fact he gave his word for abolishing marriage, in the heart, on the spot.

We have thus far traced, honestly and faithfully, the doctrine of Christ and Paul on the subject of marriage. The result is to us satisfactory. But we have yet developed only the negative view. We have found them not in favor of divorce, not polygamists, but pressing toward the cessation of marriage itself. But the question remains, as to what they expected would take the place of marriage in the posthumous, or if you please, the *angelic* state. It is distinctly said that there is no marriage there ; but the question still remains as to *what* that state is ; and in regard to it two theories may arise, and only two. The whole question lies between the Shaker doctrine, that there is no sexual relation or constitution in heaven ; and the doctrine of what may be called *pantogamy*, which recognizes the continued existence of the sexual relation, but excludes ownership, and replaces human beings where they were as children—in friendship and freedom, without selfish possession. These two are the only theories that are possible as to the resurrection state ; which state, be it remembered, Christ and his disciples adhered to as far as possible in this world, and contemplated introducing in its fullness.

We certainly have no disposition to wrest the scriptures, or misrepresent the principles of Christ and Paul in this matter. We can very readily consent to Shakerism, if that is their doctrine. All we want to know is what they really believed and taught about the resurrection state. If they saw there Shakerism, we wish to be Shakers; and if some other state of society, that form of society shall be ours. We are determined, for ourselves, *to follow hard after Paul and Christ*, and get at the soul of their intent in this thing.

But in the first place, we find no necessity whatever of a Shaker interpretation of the passage—'In the resurrection they neither marry nor are given in marriage.' The question proposed by the Sadducees evidently referred to the matter of *ownership*. Seven men had been married to one woman, and dying successively, the question was, whose she should be in the resurrection. Suppose the question had been asked in reference to slavery instead of marriage, thus: A man owning a slave dies, and leaves him to his brother: he dying, bequeaths him to the next brother : and so seven of them in succession own this slave. Now whose slave shall he be in the resurrection? This, evidently, is the amount of the Sadducees' question; and Christ's answer is as though he had said, that in the resurrection there are neither slaves nor slaveholders. It is a nullification of the idea of marriage ownership. Can any thing more be made of it ? To assume from this passage a nullification of the sexual relation, as the Shakers and others do, is as absurd as it would be to assume that, because there is no slavery, there is therefore no serving one another in the resurrection; whereas, the gospel teaches that there is more serving one another there than in the world. There is a very important distinction to be observed between the abolition of ownership and the abolition of love-relations.

While therefore, we are clear that marriage is to be abolished; it does not necessarily follow that agamy or antigamy is to take the place of it ; but on the contrary the whole spirit of the gospel in regard to service and freedom, and the whole purport of the doctrine, 'Except ye be converted and become as little children, ye shall in no wise enter the kingdom of heaven,' go far the other way : indicating that in that posthumous state which we are taught to pray for and expect on earth, the relation of the sexes will be that described in Christ's prayer—that they 'may all be one, even as I and my Father are one,' which we call pantogamy.

Recurring to the illustration with which we begun, we

may sum up and present in the shortest possible compass, the view to which the preceding examination of the Bible has led us, as follows :

Let a state of general debt, or in other words the credit-system, represent marriage. Then the divorce scheme of Owen, James and others, will be a bankrupt-law ; the poly-gamic system of the Mormons and others, will be increased speculation, or an inflation of the credit-system ; and the policy of the Shakers will be stoppage of business to avoid debt, speculation, &c.,—in other words, stagnation. Now it is conceivable that honest men should insist that all debts actually contracted shall be paid, and at the same time should be opposed to contracting debts. Such men would oppose a bankrupt-law on the one hand, and the entire credit-system on the other. It is also conceivable, that prudent men should oppose the entire credit-system, and of course dislike speci-ally any increase of speculation, while still they might be in favor of FREE BUSINESS and opposed to stagnation. So we conceive Christ and Paul, as honest and prudent men, were opposed to divorce on the one hand, and to marriage on the other; and being opposed to marriage, of course specially dis-approved of polygamy ; and yet were not Shakers, but were in favor of free social relations, to be inaugurated as soon as existing obligations could be disposed of, and the old system of bondage removed safely and peaceably.

If we have made any mistake in regard to the subsequent state to be anticipated, or the interpretation of Christ's words concerning it, the error must be shown. We shall follow Christ and Paul, let the path lead where it will. It has un-mistakably led us to the expectation that marriage is to be done away ; and the only question is, What next ? Shaker-ism, or something else ? We call for discussion. If the con-servative interpreters of the Bible, will convince us that the Shaker view is correct, relating to the posthmous state, which, (bear in mind,) we are to pray for and expect on earth, then let it be so. We shall thankfully accept anything that can be shown to be truth on this subject. In respect to their estimate of marriage, we think the Shakers nearer right than the popular churches. We agree with them in regard to the necessity of its abolishment, and the only question is as to subsequent institutions. This point, it is for the Christian world to discuss and settle. In the light which is now breaking, both from the Bible, and from reason, on the subject of marriage, all free-thinking believers will find themselves compelled to move ; and it must be either toward our position, or that of the Shakers. We can see no other alternative. Then let there be a fair investigation of the whole subject—let us ascertain if possible, the social formation that belongs to the post-mortal, or heavenly and eternal state, and all agree to accommodate ourselves thereto.

PAUL'S VIEWS OF MARRIAGE.

An Exposition of the Seventh Chapter of First Corinthians.

PRELIMINARY REMARKS.

PETER says that in Paul's epistles are 'things hard to be understood ;' and the Christian world has found that remark to be true. The seventh chapter of Romans, for instance, has been for eighteen centuries a subject of general and deplorable misapprehension. That chapter, containing the miserable confessions of a man who says, 'When I would do good, evil is present with me,' &c., has been supposed to refer to genuine Christian experience, and has been the favorite resort of persons who wanted an excuse for sin, while yet they claimed to be Christians. But it is now found that the old interpreters have misunderstood this passage, and that Paul's words have been 'wrested,' to the destruction, it is to be feared, of some who have made the most use of them. The authorities in this country and in Germany have at length discovered, and demonstrated, that it is not *Christian* experience, but *legal* experience, which Paul intended to describe in the seventh of Romans; and that Christian experience is presented in the eighth chapter, which is in perfect contrast with the seventh.

But while truth has prevailed against long-cherished error in respect to the seventh of Romans, we imagine that *the seventh chapter of 1st Corinthians* is still one of the 'hard' passages that have not been unlocked ; and one which is wrested, more or less destructively to the interests of men. It is to be hoped, however, that here too we shall at length get light, and come to a true understanding of the apostle's doctrine ;

and it may be found, in this case as in the other, that the intent of the passage has been not only perverted, but actually reversed, and turned to the opposite use from that which was intended.

Before entering upon a specific examination of this chapter on marriage, it is necessary to cast a preliminary glance at the condition and character of those to whom Paul was writing, and also at some of the general doctrines which are previously announced, and which he always taught as the constitutional principles of the gospel.

First, it is to be noticed that he was addressing a body of persons who were in a low state of spirituality. He says in the beginning of the third chapter of the epistle, " I brethren, could not speak unto you as unto spiritual, but as unto carnal, even as unto babes in Christ. I have fed you with milk and not with meat: for hitherto ye were not able to bear it; neither yet now are ye able. For ye are yet carnal." It is plain, therefore, that the whole epistle, of which this passage is the introduction, is what he calls *milk* and not *meat;* that is, it contains only such incipient disclosures of the bearing of the gospel, as are adapted to carnal persons, who are in a struggle between sin and grace, and is not intended to be a disclosure of the deep things of God, such as determine the state of the church in its ultimate, perfected condition.

'Another thing to be observed, is, that the particular discussion of the relation of the sexes in the chapter under consideration, is connected with the central subject of Paul's gospel ; viz., the *cross of Christ.* He says in the beginning of the second chapter, ' I determined not to know any thing among you, *save Jesus Christ, and him crucified.'* With such an announcement beforehand, it is to be assumed that his subsequent discourse would correspond ; and hence we are to conclude that he studied the social problem not in a random, incoherent way, but with direct reference to its connection with salvation by the cross of Christ. It becomes important then that we understand in some general way, the purport of this central doctrine about the cross of Christ, in order that we may rightly estimate the incidental deductions about marriage which are set forth in the chapter to be examined.

We have presented in the article on Constitutional Christianity, the form of truth which we understand to be designated by the term, ' the cross of Christ ;' and it is unnecessary to dwell upon it here further than to say, that Paul accepted the crucifixion of Christ as his own death and the death of all believers. Counting himself and the church as members of Christ's body, the condition of their Head necessarily passed upon them; and while immature believers might fail to fully apprehend the fact, Paul never ceased to urge it upon them, and never waived for a moment the claim on behalf of himself and the church, of being dead and risen, by virtue of the death and resurrection of Christ. He preached invariably as a man in the resurrection to a church in the resurrection. Such was the constitution of the church on the basis of the cross of Christ ; and there can be no doubt that his whole discourse in the chapter before us is shaped with reference to that idea.

The third observation necessary to be made, is, that he was preaching to a church who had been taught to expect the Second Coming of Christ *within their own lifetime.* The whole tenor of the preaching of Christ and the apostles was to this effect. The assurance everywhere accompanied the gospel, that Jesus Christ was soon to come in judgment: none knew how soon, but the period was understood to be limited within the lifetime of some of the disciples. Expectation of this event was the universal attitude of the church. In fact, Paul speaks of this expectation, in the commencement of this epistle, as follows: ' Ye come behind in no gift, *waiting for the coming of our Lord Jesus Christ,* who shall also confirm you unto the end, that ye may be blameless in the day of our Lord Jesus Christ.' As he was ' looking for the Lord Jesus Christ [to come and] change his vile body,' so he addressed the church as looking for the same glorious translation, at the appearance of Christ; and in the fifteenth chapter, speaking of that approaching event, he explicitly says, ' We shall not all sleep, but we shall all be changed.' He is not discoursing here of saints in distant ages; but of what he and they personally expected, and had a right to expect, from Christ's predictions in the twenty-fourth of Matthew and elsewhere.

A fourth point to be noticed in this preliminary view, is, that in Paul's mind, the cross of Christ, legitimately, and by virtue of the death and resurrection which it conveys to the believer, makes him free from law. ' The law hath dominion over a man as long as he liveth.' But the church, by the cross of Christ, were ' crucified to the world, and the world unto them.' They were taught to reckon themselves dead and risen; and hence, that they constituted a kingdom by themselves, beyond the jurisdiction of human judgment, and amenable in conscience, only to the spiritual authority which belongs to Christ, and the state beyond death.

An indication of this assumption in regard to their position, may be found in the beginning of the sixth chapter, where the apostle censures certain of the Corinthian church for going to law before unbelievers. While intimating that it was utterly shameful that their carnality made occasion for any disputes among them, he adjures them at least to settle such affairs by organizing courts of their own, instead of appealing to the courts of the world. He asks with astonishment, whether they were not competent to institute a judiciary among themselves, seeing that their calling as members of Christ's kingdom actually commissioned them to judge the world, and even angels. Now this assumption that they were bound to set up a judiciary among themselves to supersede courts of law in the world, was an assumption that they belonged to a distinct and independent kingdom. He recognized no other authority over them than that of Christ, and no obligation of conscience to any law but the law of Christ. This necessarily resulted from the fact of his reckoning himself dead with Christ ; for, in the language of

his definition already quoted, ' the law hath dominion over a
man [only] so long as he liveth.' It was on this ground that
the church had already repudiated the ecclesiastical law and
ordinances of Judaism; and here Paul clearly extends that
repudiation (in spirit, and in form so far as it could be done
peacefully,) to the *civil* institutions of his time.   It was his
determination to consider the church a *trans-mortal* institution—a kingdom by itself—one of ' the powers that be'—and
a candidate for judging the world.

ᴗ Whether Paul was *right* in all this, or whether he was foolish and fanatical, is quite a separate question, with which we
are not at present concerned.   What we want, is not to settle
the right or wrong of the positions he assumed and the course
he took, but to ascertain precisely what his position and course
were.   If on fair examination of his views about the cross
of Christ and the Second Coming, any persons choose to
think that they are wiser than he was in his deductions, there
will of course be opportunity to differ; it is sufficient for us
now to be able to say, such evidently were *his* views on these
subjects.

We will now present the whole of the 7th chapter of 1Cor-
inthians, together with the part of the 6th immediately
preceding, which will be found important in connection, as
disclosing the foundation principles of what follows.   We present it in the common English translation ; and such correc-
tions as we have to make in the rendering, as also the explana-
tory remarks which we shall offer on the 'hard things' that
occur, we will place in after-notes, referring to numbers in the
text.   The reader, if he wishes to *study* our exposition, is ad-
vised, in reading the Bible extract following, to stop when he
meets with a figure, and turn over to the corresponding figure
in our notes.

—

First Corinthians, from Chapter 6: 12, to the end of Chapter 7.

" All things are lawful unto me, but all things are not expedient : all
things are lawful for me, but I will not be brought under the power of
any. (1) Meats for the belly, and the belly for meats : but God shall de-

stroy both it and them. Now the body is not for fornication, but for the Lord; and the Lord for the body. And God hath both raised up the Lord, and will also raise up us by his own power. (2) Know ye not that your bodies are the members of Christ? shall I then take the members of Christ, and make them the members of an harlot? God forbid! What! know ye not that he which is joined to an harlot is one body? for two, saith he, shall be one flesh. But he that is joined unto the Lord is one spirit. Flee fornication. Every sin that a man doeth, is without the body; but he that committeth fornication, sinneth against his own body. What! know ye not that your body is the temple of the Holy Ghost which is in you, which ye have of God, and ye are not your own? For ye are bought with a price: therefore glorify God in your body, [and in your spirit, which are God's.]" (3)

"Now concerning the things whereof ye wrote unto me: It is good for a man not to touch a woman. Nevertheless, to avoid fornication, let every man have his own wife, and let every woman have her own husband. (4) Let the husband render unto the wife due benevolence: and likewise also the wife unto the husband. The wife hath not power of her own body, but the husband: and likewise also the husband hath not power of his own body, but the wife. (5) Defraud ye not one the other, except it be with consent for a time, that ye may give yourselves to fasting and prayer; and come together again, that Satan tempt you not for your incontinency. (6) But I speak this by permission, and not of commandment. For I would that all men were even as I myself. But every man hath his proper gift of God, one after this manner, and another after that. I say therefore to the unmarried and widows, it is good for them if they abide even as I. But if they cannot contain, let them marry: for it is better to marry than to burn. (7) And unto the married I command, yet not I, but the Lord, Let not the wife depart from her husband; but and if she depart, let her remain unmarried, or be reconciled to her husband: (8) and let not the husband put away his wife. But to the rest speak I, not the Lord: If any brother hath a wife that believeth not, and she be pleased to dwell with him, let him not put her away. And the woman which hath an husband that believeth not, and if he be pleased to dwell with her, let her not leave him. For the unbelieving husband is sanctified by the wife, and the unbelieving wife is sanctified by the husband: else were your children unclean; but now are they holy. But if the unbelieving depart, let him depart. A brother or a sister is not under bondage in such cases; but God hath called us to peace. For what knowest thou, O wife, whether thou shalt save thy husband? or how knowest thou, O man, whether thou shalt save thy wife? But as God hath distributed to every man, as the Lord hath called every one, so let him walk. (9) And so ordain I in all churches. Is any man called being circumcised? let him not become uncircumcised. Is any called in uncircumcision? let him not be circumcised. Circumcision is nothing, and uncircumcision is nothing, but the keeping of the commandments of God. (10) Let every man abide in the same calling wherein he was called. Art thou called being a servant? care not for it; but if thou mayest be made free, use it rather. (11) For he that is called in the Lord, being a servant, is the Lord's freeman: likewise also he that is called, being free, is Christ's servant. Ye are bought with a price; be not ye the servants of men. (12) Brethren, let every man, wherein he is called, therein abide with God. Now concerning virgins, I have no commandment of the Lord: yet I give my judgment as one that hath obtained mercy of the Lord to be faithful. I suppose therefore that this is good for the present distress; (13) I say that it is good for a man so to be. Art thou bound unto a wife? seek not to be loosed: Art thou loosed from a wife? seek not a wife. But and if thou marry, thou hast not sinned: and if a virgin marry, she hath not sinned. Nevertheless, such shall have trouble in the flesh; but I spare you. (14) But this I say, brethren, the time is short. (15) It remaineth, that both they that have wives, be as though they had none; and they that weep, as though they wept not; and they that rejoice, as though they rejoiced not; and they that buy, as though they possessed not; and they that use this world, as not abusing it. For the fashion of this world passeth away. (16) But I would have you without carefulness. He that is unmarried careth for the things that belong to the Lord, how he may please the Lord; but he that is married careth for the things that are of the world, how he may please his wife. (17) There is difference also between a wife and a virgin. The unmarried woman careth for the things of the Lord, that she may be holy, both in body and in spirit: but she that is married, careth for the things of the world, how she may please her husband. And this I speak for your own profit; not that I may cast a snare upon you, but for that which is comely, and that ye may attend upon the Lord without distraction. (18) But if any man think that he behaveth himself uncomely toward his virgin, if she pass the flower of her age, and need so require, let him do what he will, he sinneth not: let them marry. Nevertheless, he that standeth steadfast in his heart, having no necessity, but hath power over his own will, and hath so decreed in his heart that he will keep his virgin, doeth well. So then he that giveth her in marriage doeth well; but he that giveth her not in marriage doeth better. (19) The wife is bound by the law as long as her husband liveth; but if her husband be dead, she is at liberty to be married to whom she will; only in the Lord. (20) But she is happier if she so abide, after my judgment: and I think also that I have the Spirit of God."

—

NOTES.

(1.) '*All things are lawful unto me.*'—This declaration, which is several times repeated in Paul's epistles, is plainly connected with his theory of the emancipation of believers from all human law, and their transfer to the *spiritual* government of Christ. As he directed the Corinthians to renounce reference to the civil tribunals of the world, and to establish courts of their own, so he also sought to put out of their consciences, individually, all reference to any human law whatsoever ; and in the place of it, set them upon judging their condition solely with reference to their relation to Christ and the interests of their spiritual nature. But a bad use could be made of that emancipation ; and doubtless there was a degree of perverse antinomianism in the church, which led to an extravagant estimate of their independence by their connection with Christ and death to the law. Too much account was made of the principle, and not enough of its limitations. Hence while Paul admits and reiterates it as a true doctrine that ' all things are lawful,' he also proceeds to enforce the counter considerations—'All things are not expedient'—'I will not be brought under the power of any.' We find, however, that in the counsel that follows, he does not turn their consciences at all toward human law ; but even in censuring fornication he adheres faithfully to his first principle, and condemns that offense, not because it was unlawful, but because it was spiritually pernicious and contrary to their relations to Christ.

(2) '*Meats for the belly, and the belly for meats; but God shall destroy both it and them. Now the body is not for fornication, but for the Lord ; and the Lord for the body.—And God hath both raised up the Lord, and will also raise up us by his own power.*'—Here are obviously two principles presented in contrast, and their different results. ' Meats for the belly, and the belly for meats,' is one principle : ' The body is for the Lord, and the Lord for the body,' is another and quite opposite principle. The results of the two are correspondingly opposite. In the one case, ' the Lord shall destroy both it [the body] and them, [meats,]' and in the other case, God raises up ' both the Lord and us.'

It is evident that Paul does not intend to sanction the first
principle, but presents it, (probably, as a current Epicurean
maxim,) for the sake of showing its result, and giving point to
his antithesis. The idea is, if you hold that the body is for carnal enjoyment, and choose to marry it in the downward way
to matter, you will have your end in destruction. The same
sentiment occurs, in quite similar language, in Phil. 3: 18, 19.
On the other hand, the principle which he *sanctions* is, that
'the body is for the Lord, and the Lord for the body,' and
the result of this marriage is resurrection. We shall find in
this latter doctrine the secret thread of all that follows—the
clue to his meaning in all that he says about the intercourse
of the sexes. He proceeds to condemn fornication, not because it is unlawful, or on the ordinary ground of morality,
but because it withdraws the body from its true owner, the
Lord; and we shall see afterwards that his objection to marriage stands on the same ground.

(3) '*Glorify God in your body,* [*and in your spirit, which
are God's.*]—The last clause of this verse, which we have
placed in brackets, is not found in many of the original manu-
scripts ; and, according to the best authorities, is spurious.
There is evident reason for that conclusion, discoverable in
the text itself. Paul had been insisting that the believer's
body belongs to the Lord, and should be married to him exclusively ; and as the close of a powerful argument on this
point, the exhortation is exceedingly appropriate—'*Therefore*
glorify God in your *body.*' The addition about the 'spirit'
appears common-place and uncalled-for in this connection,
and serves rather to weaken the force of the sentiment. It
would seem to have been added by persons who either did not
understand Paul, or chose to round off his period at the
expense of his idea.

'Glorify God in your *body.*' This was the point which he
wished to enforce ; and the whole passage corresponds with a
similar one in Romans, where he says : 'I beseech you therefore, brethren, by the mercies of God, that ye present your

bodies a living sacrifice, holy, acceptable unto God.' We must clearly appreciate him on this point in order to understand his doctrine about fornication, and also his subsequent position in respect to marriage. He preached Christ crucified and risen, and constantly assumed that by spiritual union with him, believers too were dead and risen ; whereby they entered into new relations throughout, both of body and soul. Christ, he alleged, had ' apprehended' them as in the resurrection, and this was henceforth their true marriage relation. All their experience and discipline was to enable them ' to apprehend that for which they were apprehended of Christ Jesus,' viz., the full realization in body, as well as in spirit, (see Phil. 3: 11,) of the resurrection state. With a clear understanding of this point of his theology, we shall have no difficulty in understanding his discourse upon marriage in the chapter which we now enter upon.

(4.) ' *It is good for a man not to touch a woman. Nevertheless, to avoid fornication, let every man have his own wife, and let every woman have her own husband.'*—The apostle's previous principle that ' the body is for the Lord,' makes ground for him now to assume the more general position, that ' it is good for a man not to touch a woman' at all ; which is opposed to marriage-commerce as really as to fornication.—Paul was clearly opposed to both—in different *degrees*, it is true ; but for precisely the same reason, viz., that both interfere with the integrity of believers' relations to the Lord.—Their bodies were not for human possession, either in the way of marriage or prostitution ; but ' for the Lord.' We see however, as has been said, that he estimated the two things differently ; and that when called to choose between them, he preferred the recognized institution of marriage, to any looser mode of alliance. Fornication, in his view, while it had in it all the bad elements of marriage, tending to withdraw men from Christ, their true husband, had also additional evils connected with it, which made it far more destructive to their spiritual interests. For instance, it is obvious that it would

almost necessarily have brought them into association with the
profligate and abandoned, and would have led to various dis-
turbances in their civil and social relations.   Hence, as the
wisest choice of evils, Paul advises them to avoid fornication
by marriage.   It is not to be understood by this, that he
meant to recommend marriage to all, without qualification,
but simply, *if it was necessary* in order to avoid irregular
courses, that they should marry, and each one have his own
partner. (See 1 Tim. 5: 11—14, where Paul recommends that
‘ the *younger* women’ should marry for reasons of this kind.)
But the state which he prefers to marriage, is intimated
in the first clause, where he says, ‘ It is good for a man
not to touch a woman;’ viz., a state of entire freedom from
sexual ties.   That was the high ground on which he stood
.personally, ˙and the one which he could recommend to all, as
believers in Christ, counting themselves dead and risen, and
their bodies belonging to the Lord.

(5) ‘ *The wife hath not power of her own body, but the hus-*
band: and likewise also the husband hath not power of his own
body, but the wife.’—In the previous verse there is a debt spoken of as due between married parties, and this verse discloses
what that debt is.   In the marriage contract the parties mu-
tually make over to each other the right of their bodies: and
here comes out clearly the point of Paul’s objection to the institution.   He cannot recommend such a sale; though he insists that if the sale has taken place, the terms of it shall be
faithfully adhered to.   In a previous verse, when he said, ‘All
things are lawful to me,’ he added, ‘*I will not be brought un-*
der the power of any.’ Here he says, that by marriage the
man comes personally under the *power* of his wife; and the
woman under the power of her husband.   This is the nature
of the contract.   But having taken the position that our
bodies are for the Lord—that we are bought with a price, and
are bound to glorify him freely in body as well as soul—it is a
matter of course that he should object to any relation which
brings the body under the power of another, as marriage does.

It was contrary to the constitutional principles of the gospel; and for his part, '*he* would not be brought under the power of any.' If others could not *keep* their freedom as he did, he thought the best surrender they could make was by marriage. But in principle, the making over of their persons to another by marriage, was as really a breach of their assumed relation to Christ as fornication, though not so destructive.

(6) '*Defraud ye not one the other, except it be with consent for a time, that ye may give yourselves to fasting and prayer; and come together again, that Satan tempt you not for your incontinency.*'—He assumes that persons who find it necessary to marry to avoid fornication—so compromising in some degree their relations to Christ—are *incontinent* persons; and his directions to them are such as good sense would suggest in view of that fact. After placing themselves in the intimate relationship of marriage, he judges that their only safe way is to live according to the terms of the institution. Not to pay their debts would be to expose them to more difficulty than any other course, and his idea in substance is, that if they have adopted marriage as a resource against temptation, they ought to make it their *security*, and the orderly vent of their passion, rather than by any notions of abstinence, expose themselves to further difficulties from incontinency.

(7) '*For I would that all men were even as I myself. But every man hath his proper gift of God, one after this manner, and another after that. I say therefore to the unmarried and widows, it is good for them to abide even as I. But if they cannot contain, let them marry; for it is better to marry than to burn.*'—Here marriage is again distinctly placed on the ground of a choice of evils. Paul himself was unmarried, and he repeats emphatically the wish that all believers stood with him in that respect.

We have then, thus far, three sexual relations set forth, with a clear gradation of preference in the apostle's mind: one which he utterly condemns, viz., fornication,—one which he tolerates under circumstances of necessity, but with objections, viz., marriage,—and one which he approves of, viz., a state of entire freedom from unspiritual institutions and obligations.

(8) '*Let not the wife depart from her husband: but and if she depart, let her remain unmarried, or be reconciled to her husband.*'—Here the idea is badly confused, by a defective translation. As the text stands, it would seem that after strictly commanding married persons, in the name of the Lord, not to separate, he then gives them liberty to separate, by proposing an alternative. This inconsistency does not exist in the original; but is made in the translation by a false rendering of the word for ' depart,' in the second case where it occurs; which is in the past tense, and should read 'departed,' or 'have departed.' Then the apostle's meaning is simple and clear. He commands those who are married not to depart; but if in any case separation *has* taken place previously—if the wife *have departed*, then he says let her either remain unmarried or go back and be reconciled to her husband.

(9) '*If any brother hath a wife that believeth not, and she be pleased to dwell with him, let him not put her away. And the woman which hath an husband that believeth not, and if he be pleased to dwell with her, let her not leave him.....But if the unbelieving depart, let him depart. A brother or a sister is not under bondage in such cases.....But as God hath distributed to every man, as the Lord hath called every one, so let him walk.*'—The order against voluntary divorce was very peremptory and unqualified. While Paul objected on general principles to marriage, yet in any case where that contract had been assumed, he opposed the violation of it. The policy of Christ seems to have taken the direction of not disturbing existing relations of any kind—and this policy took effect in the case of marriage precisely as it did in the case of circumcision and slavery, which Paul introduced afterwards as illustrations. Three times in the passage from the tenth verse to the twenty-fourth, the order is given, ' Stand as you are !'

'.Whether you are circumcised or uncircumcised, stand as you are. Whether you are a slave or a freeman, stand as you are. Whether you are married or unmarried, stand as you are—*if you can.*' So Paul ordained in all the churches.

(10) '*Circumcision is nothing, and uncircumcision is nothing, but the keeping of the commandments of God.*'—From the subject-matter of this chapter, and the whole connection of his argument, we cannot but conclude that this is intended to express precisely his principle in respect to marriage. So far as conscience is concerned, (he would say,) marriage is nothing, and celibacy is nothing ; but a state of exclusive devotion to the Lord is every thing. That is the marriage, and the only marriage, that the true believer in Christ recognizes as at the bottom of his existence. His external state with reference to the various institutions of men, is a matter of comparative indifference, to be left to the control of expediency, while he gives sole attention to loyalty to God.

(11) '*Art thou called, being a servant ? care not for it : but if thou mayest be made free, use it rather.*'—This is evidently an exact parallel of his advice respecting marriage, and an illustration of the same principle. He finds that the best state for a believer is one of freedom ; but if in any case persons found themselves captives of existing institutions, they were not to count it incompatible with their relations to Christ, or seek to free themselves in a violent way. Their expectation of the coming of Christ to break all their earthly bonds, was undoubtedly the element which kept them steady under this policy of passive conformity.

(12) '*Ye are bought with a price; be not ye the servants of men.*'—This, in a little different form, is the same idea with that at the beginning, where he says, 'The body is for the Lord,' and is the hinge and underlying principle of the whole discourse. By the very constitution of the gospel, believers knew no owner or master but Christ ; and in all their subjection to the laws and ordinances of men, they were radically obeying, not men, but Christ. Paul knew them only in that

relation, and exhorted them to have no other master at heart. So far as Christ directed them, they were to pay regard to the outward institutions of the time, not, however, out of respect or conscientious obligation to those institutions, but purely from respect to Christ, whose pleasure it was that they should comply. Whether as slaves or as citizens, as Jews or as Greeks, married or unmarried, they were to do every thing ' as unto the Lord'—'in the name of the Lord Jesus.' The principle of their sole allegiance to Christ was always present in Paul's mind, and was the essence of his doctrine of conformity. He had found a way of conforming peaceably to the ordinances of this world, yet without being subject to them—a way in which a man could be a faithful servant, and yet keep his interior independence, and serve only the Lord. In strict truth, there was a sort of righteous *duplicity* taught in the church, in respect to human institutions, and Paul was particularly an adept in it. His principles, while they would make men peaceable citizens, exemplary in conforming to all the circumstances of the society they were in, would after all not leave an atom of loyalty in their hearts for the institutions of the world, but would turn all their devotion, both of conscience and affection, to the kingdom of Christ.

(13) '*I suppose that this is good for the present distress.*'— The popular method of disposing of the whole chapter, refers its meaning to the ' present distress' spoken of in this verse; and supposes that expression to allude to some peculiarity of the circumstances of that particular time, as war or persecution, which made occasion for Paul to think it not advisable to marry. But we have seen, and shall see hereafter, that he places his objections to marriage on entirely other grounds than those which this interpretation suggests. Furthermore, if we go back to the 4th chapter of this epistle, (verse 8,) we find that the Corinthian church was in no particular outward distress of any kind, but rather in luxurious prosperity. It would seem from the account of them there given, that they

were in as good situation for marriage as people ever were.—
Hence it cannot be true that he referred to any necessity of
an outward kind, belonging specially to their time and circumstances. The necessity or distress which he had in mind,
as appears from what follows, was the state of trial and labor
in overcoming the world, intervening between their first faith
in Christ as their resurrection-head, and the Second Coming
which was near at hand, when their resurrection with him
was to be perfected. That interval was a period of distress
and necessity—a time of conflict in which the flesh was to be
subdued under the spirit—a period when they were to work
themselves out of the spirit and fashion of this world, and
prepare themselves for their final marriage with Christ. It
was simply the necessity which is involved in the Christian
struggle for regeneration; and such as every one is in who has
undertaken to overcome the world and receive Christ. It was
in view of the exigencies of this spiritual enterprise—the presenting of themselves faultless in the resurrection—that Paul
urged the doctrine that the body is for the Lord, and wished
them free, not only from fornication, but also from marriage.

(14) '*If thou marry, thou hast not sinned: and if a virgin
marry, she hath not sinned. Nevertheless such shall have
trouble in the flesh.*'—Having treated previously of married
persons, the apostle is here considering the case of the unmarried, or virgins. And now, as before, he refuses to treat the
subject as a matter of law, or conscience, and discriminates
only between expediencies. It is perfectly lawful to marry—
'all things are lawful'— but 'it is not expedient,' because,
marriage insures 'trouble in the flesh.'

It is worth while to consider for a moment, what is meant
by this last expression. We naturally refer for an explanation, to the definition of marriage, in the beginning of the
chapter. 'The wife hath not power of her own body, but the
husband: and likewise also, the husband hath not power of
his own body, but the wife.' Marriage being a mutual sale
of persons, you put the power of your own body into another's

hands, and of course, there will be 'trouble in the flesh.'—
The man will have trouble from incontinent passion, and the
woman from child-bearing. Paul did not consider this 'trouble'
which attends and follows marriage, as any thing to be depre-
cated. Indeed, it was in accordance with the general doctrine and means of grace in other cases. When a person was
utterly unmanageable by ordinary influences, he was ' delivered
to Satan, for the *destruction* of the flesh, that the spirit might
be saved.' So Paul would say, " If a person is incontinent,
and cannot give his body to the Lord, let him give his spirit
to the Lord, and his body to marriage: he will then have
' trouble in the flesh' that will reduce his body, so that the
matter will come out right at last."

(15) *'But this I say, brethren, the time is short.'*—What is
the short time that Paul has here in view? Evidently, the
interval previous to the crisis mentioned immediately after, in the same connection, where he says, ' the fashion of
this world passeth away.' That was the event that was to
come in a short time; and there can be no doubt that it was
the Second Coming. There are multitudes of passages, in
which the coming of Christ is alluded to in a similar way, as
a basis of exhortation to sobriety and separation from the
world.

(16) ' *It remaineth, that both they that have wives be as
though they had none; and they that weep, as though they wept
not; and they that rejoice, as though they rejoiced not; and
they that buy, as though they possessed not; and they that use
this world, as not abusing it; for the fashion of this world
passeth away.'*—On the principle by which those who were
slaves were enjoined not to be the servants of men, the apostle now exhorts persons involved in marriage, and in the
property system of the world, to hold these relations lightly,
and be in heart as though they were free. He counselled
them in respect to all these worldly claims, as we have said
above, to an honest duplicity: that while they conformed to
them in externals, peacefully for the present, they should

transfer all their real loyalty to Christ and the immortal state, which they were shortly to enter at his promised coming. A new heavens and new earth were immediately before them, in connection with that event, and of course, an end of the whole fashion and arrangement of this world. In Christ's declaration about the resurrection, Matt. 22: 30, they had explicit ground for the expectation that marriage, at least, should be abolished; hence there was a peculiar appropriateness in all Paul's advice on the subject. He gives as a reason for their incipient repudiation of marriage, that 'the fashion of this world passeth away.' It would have been simply an equivalent reason, to have assigned the saying of Christ, that 'in the resurrection they neither marry, nor are given in marriage.'

Here the fact should be distinctly noted that Paul does not undertake to describe what was to come *after* the fashion of this world had passed away. He gives advice appropriate to the short time previous to that crisis, but does not go beyond it. We must assume that it was to be the ushering in of an entirely different state of things from that which they were then in ; but what the particulars were to be, he does not say. All that we can know from what goes before, is that in that heavenly state the Lord is the husband of the church, individually and collectively ; that his right to their souls and to their bodies supersedes all the rights which marriage gives ; and that in comparison with marriage, which conveys to another a person's power over himself, that state is one of perfect freedom.

We must further bear in mind that the apostle is here addressing carnal men, to whom he had said distinctly that they could not bear the deep things of God, the 'strong meat' of the gospel, but only the milk of primary, incipient truth. He had in his own heart wisdom which he spoke only among the perfect. (Chap. 2: 6.) He had been in the third heavens, and there heard things which he could not disclose to them at all— (2 Cor. 12: 4)—things which related, we may presume, to the

sequel of that crisis that was before the church, when the
fashion of this world should have passed away. But he does
not reveal, in any direct terms, these deeper mysteries. His
expectations of that future state are only to be sought out
by inference, and reasoning from the *hints* which he gives us,
and from, the nature of things.

We have in the passage now before us a hint in regard to
the change that was to come in property arrangements. 'Let
those that buy be as though they possessed not; and they
that use this world as not abusing it: for the fashion of this
world passeth away.' Buying and selling and selfish possession, is an institution of this world like marriage, which was
to pass away. On the day of Pentecost, it did pass away,
for the time being, in the church, so that 'neither said any
of them, that aught of the things which he possessed was his
own, but they distributed to every man as he had need, and
had all things common.' This affords a glimpse, we think,
of a permanent after-state of the church, in respect to property, when the fashion of buying and selling would pass away.
A parallel inference in respect to buying and selling persons
in marriage, is inevitably suggested by the connected clause,
'Let those that have wives be as though they had none, &c.

(17) '*He that is unmarried careth for the things that belong to
the Lord, how he may please the Lord: but he that is married
careth for the things that are of the world, how he may please
his wife.*'—The apostle has constant reference to the primary
idea that ' the body is for *the Lord,*' and here, in addition to
his previous objection to the marriage-sale, he points out the
spiritual consequence ; viz. that the married care for the
things of the world, how they may please each other, and not
the Lord. It is evident that this objection, in his mind, was
a fundamental and perpetual one against the working of the
institution, and had no reference whatever to any special in-
convenience then pressing upon the church. His reasoning
in this verse must always have its full bearing so long as the
believer is in a condition to need freedom from care, that he

may give himself to God—so long as he is in conflict with the world, and requires discipline of spirit to hold him in loyalty to Christ. Whenever and wherever he is in any degree liable to be turned away by the things of this world, these principles are pertinent and necessary.

(18) '*And this I speak for your own profit; not that I may cast a snare upon you, but for that which is comely, and that ye may attend upon the Lord without distraction.*'—He would have all believers in a state of exclusive attention to Christ—so earnestly bent on giving themselves, body and soul to him, that they would not entangle themselves with any other obligations.

(19) '*So then he that giveth in marriage, doeth well; but he that giveth not in marriage, doeth better.*'—The apostle is here treating, either the case of a parent having daughters, or, (which is more probable,) the case of young persons who are 'engaged.' He simply repeats the advice which he had already given, recommending one course as the best, but permitting another as lawful. He would put them under no constraint of conscience about the matter.

(20) '*She is at liberty to be married to whom she will; only in the Lord.*'—Here Paul excludes all marriage with unbelievers as decidedly as he forbids fornication. If persons find it necessary to marry, it is to be only within the church. There is no license whatever in his morality, for intermarriage between the church and the world.

—

CONCLUDING REMARKS.

Let us now sum up what is before us :

1. We have the general doctrine that the body is for the Lord.

2. Fornication is vehemently condemnned as the worst violation of that principle.

3. Marriage is tolerated as a refuge from fornication; but is treated as a snare and a diversion from Christ, to be avoided if possible.

4. Voluntary abandonment of marriage obligations already contracted, is prohibited.

5. Marriage with unbelievers is prohibited.

6. Interior conformity to the claims of marriage is prohibited.

7. These doctrines about marriage are not based on any temporary circumstances, but on the nature of the marriage contract and relation, which gives men and women the ownership of each other, to the damage of Christ's ownership.

8. We have allusions to an ultimate state, expected as near by the church, when their 'present distress' would terminate, not in marriage, but in entire freedom from the fashion of the world.

All these ideas may be brought together and presented in their true connection, by substituting in our minds the idea of slavery for that of marriage, thus: Suppose that a body of persons living in a slave-territory, and involved in slavery as owners or slaves, are called by a deliverer who has come among them, to emigrate at a period not far distant, to a land of freedom. And suppose that in addition to the usual laws of slavery, the government they are under makes it criminal for any one to employ free labor;—which supposition is necessary to make the case parallel with that of marriage, since the law of marriage prohibits connexion of the sexes without marriage. Such being the circumstances, the advice of the deliverer, if he were as wise as Paul, would be as follows: "Avoid breaking the law. If any of you cannot live without servants, buy them. But the better way is to get along without help, rather than entangle yourselves with slavery. If you buy servants, buy only those who are in sympathy with our project of emigration, and treat them not as servants, but as brethren.— Let those who are slaves, be obedient and faithful: let there be no running away, even from masters who have no connection with our enterprise. Let all remain quiet and peaceable, and bide their time. We shall soon be in a land of freedom."

Such seems to us to be the tone and drift of Paul's counsels about marriage.

We are not responsible for those counsels, and might content ourselves with simply being honest in bringing them to light, without endorsing them. But we are free to say in conclusion, that, for our part, we think Paul was right in his views of the Gospel and of Marriage; and we accept his counsels and practical principles, heartily believing that (with such variations of details as he himself would have made, if he had lived eighteen hundred years after the Second Coming, and the time had come for *abolition* instead of *emigration*) they are wise and good for all who have a higher object than that of perpetuating their race; viz., the attainment of eternal life for themselves.

8

THE LAW OF ADULTERY.

A SPECIMEN OF CHRIST'S MORAL PHILOSOPHY.

THE Bible brings to view *two species of adultery*, viz: the ordinary crime of trespass on the rights secured by marriage, which is the only adultery known to human law ; and the crime of worldliness or sin, which is reckoned as adultery, because it is a violation of the marriage-rights of God, who justly claims the whole heart of man.   The propriety of treating this latter crime as adultery, results from the assumption which every where appears in the Bible, that the rightful union of God with man is a marriage relation—i. e., a relation which is exclusive, perpetual, and supremely sacred, according to the demand of the law, *'Thou shalt love the Lord thy God with all thy heart.'*   Such language as the following is common in the Old Testament :—*'As a wife treacherously departeth from her husband, so have ye dealt treacherously with me, O house of Israel, saith the Lord.'*   Jer. 3: 20.— (See also Isa. 54: 4, 5. 62: 4, 5. Jer. 31: 31, 32.— Ezek. 16: &c.)   In the New Testament, James, with obvious reference to divine and not human rights, addresses the double-minded in the church as *'adulterers* and *abulteresses,'* asking them, appropriately, if they were not aware *'that the friendship of the world is enmity with God ?'* *'Whosoever,'* says he, *'will be a friend of the world, is an enemy of God;'* i. e., he is an adulterer against the divine marriage relation. Jas. 4: 4. (See also Rom. 7: 4. Eph. 5: 23—32. Rev. 19: 7. &c.)

Sin, in every form, is of course unfaithfulness to the marriage covenant of God; but the generic sin called ' the love of the world,' or ' the love of money,' (which Paul says is the ' root of all evil,') is evidently treated by James and others as the special indictable crime of adultery under the higher law.

As we are bound, then, by the Bible, (which certainly is the best authority on all questions of law,) to recognize two kinds of adultery; and as it is desirable to distinguish them, according to their respective natures, as above defined, we will call the infraction of *human* rights of marriage the *lower adultery;* and ' the love of the world,' whereby God's marital rights are dishonored, the *higher adultery.*

In respect to the comparative enormity of these two crimes, we invite attention to the following *expose* of the views of Jesus Christ, the Chief Justice of Christianity, which we have compiled from the reports of the four Evangelists.

CHRIST'S VIEW OF THE LOWER ADULTERY.

1. He repeated in one instance the law, '*Thou shalt not commit adultery,*' in connection with the other commands of the decalogue. Matt. 19 : 18.

2. He mentioned adultery among the sins which proceed from the heart. Matt. 15: 19.

3. He gave a new definition of adultery, which greatly extended the purview of the law, and the area of transgression. ' Ye have heard,' he says, ' that it was said by them of old time, Thou shalt not commit adultery. But I say unto you, that whosoever looketh on a woman to lust after her, hath committed adultery with her already in his heart. ' Matt. 5 : 27, 28.

4. He reformed the jurisprudence of divorce, in such a manner as to bring practices which had been popular, and were even tolerated by Moses, within the scope of the law against adultery. He recognized fornication only as a proper cause of divorce. With this exception, he gave a positive and inflexible law against divorce, in these words:—'Whosoever shall put away his wife and marry another, committeth adultery against her: and if a woman shall put away her husband, and be married to another, she committeth adultery.' Mark 10: 11, 12. Matt. 5: 31, 32, &c.

These are all the observations of the Chief Justice on the subject of the lower adultery which we find in the reports.

We discover from them that he was a rigorous, logical inter-
preter of the law ; and that in his view adultery is a vastly
more extensive vice than was imagined by the Jews, or is
imagined generally at the present day.

It should be observed, however, that the opinions and
arguments we have noticed, relate solely to the meaning and
extent of *the law,* and not at all to the *degree of the offense,*
or the amount of condemnation and punishment that should
be awarded to it. It remains therefore, to ascertain as well
as we can from hints and facts, (since direct *dicta* on this
point are not to be found,) what Christ's opinion was of the
enormity and desert of the lower adultery. After faithful
search, we find only the four following items of indirect evidence on this point, which must pass for what they are
worth.

1. A woman, taken in the act of adultery, was brought
before Christ by his legalist adversaries, for judgment. He
shrewdly managed, as her counsel, to obtain for her an acquit-
tal from her accusers, and then, as her judge, discharged her,
saying—' Neither do I condemn thee ; go, and sin no more.'
John 8 : 3—11.

2. We may fairly infer what would have been his treatment
of a *male* transgressor of the seventh commandment, from his
story of the prodigal son. The young man had spent his substance ' *among harlots ;*' but he was welcomed home by his
father without being called to account particularly for that
part of his offense—and apparently with the approbation of
Christ. Luke 15 : 11, &c.

3. One of Christ's female favorites (who indeed can be identified with much probability as Mary, the sister of Lazarus,)
had been a public ' sinner,' i. e., undoubtedly, an adulteress
or harlot. (See Luke 7: 37—50; and compare John 11: 2.)
Another, viz. Mary Magdalene, (' out of whom went seven
devils,') was probably of the same character. Luke 8: 2.

4. The woman of Samaria, who drew forth one of Christ's
most interesting discourses, was living in adultery at the

time. He detected and mentioned the fact, but without breaking fellowship or expressing displeasure. His disciples marveled that he talked with her, but he preached the gospel to her liberally, and made her the honored instrument of a great revival in her native village. John 4.

This is all the evidence we have of Christ's views of the enormity and desert of the lower adultery.

It should be mentioned in this connection, that ordinary adultery was certainly very prevalent among the Jews in Christ's time. This is indicated by the withdrawal of every one of the woman's accusers when Christ said to them, ' Let him that is without sin cast the first stone;' and also by the expression used by Christ—'a wicked and *adulterous* generation.' So that there was plenty of occasion, if Christ had been disposed, for rebuking and anathematizing this particular sin. Yet we do not find an instance of his manifesting special displeasure against it.

To sum up the results of this review—Christ, as an expounder of law, went far beyond the public opinion of his time, in extending the *scope* of the command against adultery : but he fell far short of public opinion in his estimate of the *degree* of the crime : or more briefly, he magnified the law of adultery till every body stood guilty before it ; but when he came to pass sentence on the convicts, he gave judgment for mere nominal damages.

CHRIST'S VIEW OF THE HIGHER ADULTERY.

We get our definition of the higher adultery from such passages as the following :—' Ye adulterers and adulteresses, know ye not that the friendship of the world is enmity with God ? Whosoever therefore will be a friend of the world, is an enemy of God.' Jas. 4: 4. ' If any man love the world, the love of the Father is not in him.' 1 John 2: 15. ' The love of money is the root of all evil.' 1Tim. 6: 10. ' Ye cannot serve God and Mammon.' Matt. 6: 24.

Worldliness in the common acceptation of the term, or more specifically, that method of life which Dr. Franklin recom-

mended by example and proverbs, is certainly the precise vice
aimed at in these passages and branded as an entire breach of
the higher marriage contract, i. e., adultery.

It is evident that no serious distinction is made in these
passages, between *different kinds* of worldliness ; as for instance, between honest and dishonest, scrupulous and unscru-
pulous worldliness. The essence of the crime of adultery, in
the higher as well as in the lower form, consists in withdrawing the affections from the rightful husband, and giving them
—no matter how honestly or decently—to a paramour.

It may be said that the higher adultery is a vice *of the
heart,* and cannot therefore be treated as a crime, like common adultery, which is an overt act. But it should be observed that in the jurisprudence of Christ, the lower adultery
is treated as a vice of the heart, as we have seen ; so that no
important distinction can be raised on this ground. Both
kinds of adultery are primarily vices of the heart, and both
are completed in overt acts.

The opinions of the Chief Justice on the higher adultery,
as recorded by the evangelists, are very decided and copious.
We shall not be able, in our limited space, to exhaust the
subject by citations, as we did in the case of the lower adultery. We will confine ourselves to a selection of the most
prominent observations of Christ, relating to the crime under
consideration.

In one of his earliest and most important charges—the Ser-
mon on the Mount—he went into a minute dissection and
faithful denunciation of the higher adultery, (which may be
designated at the present day as Franklinism,) and laid down
the law on the subject as follows :

"Lay not up for yourselves treasures upon earth, where moth and rust
doth corrupt, and where thieves break through and steal: but lay up for
yourselves treasures in heaven, where neither moth nor rust doth corrupt,
and where thieves do not break through nor steal. For where your treasure is, there will your heart be also. The light of the body is the eye: if
therefore thine eye be single, thy whole body shall be full of light. But
if thine eye be evil, thy whole body shall be full of darkness. If there-

fore the light that is in thee be darkness, how great is that darkness! No man can serve two masters: for either he will hate the one, and love the other; or else he will hold to the one, and despise the other. Ye cannot serve God and Mammon. Therefore I say unto you, Take no thought for your life, what ye shall eat, or what ye shall drink: nor yet for your body, what ye shall put on. Is not the life more than meat, and the body than raiment? Behold the fowls of the air: for they sow not, neither do they reap, nor gather into barns: yet your heavenly Father feedeth them.— Are ye not much better than they? Which of you by taking thought can add one cubit unto his stature? And why take ye thought for raiment? Consider the lilies of the field, how they grow; they toil not, neither do they spin: And yet I say unto you, that even Solomon in all his glory, was not arrayed like one of these. Wherefore, if God so clothe the grass of the field, which to-day is, and to-morrow is cast into the oven, shall he not much more clothe you, O ye of little faith? Therefore, take no thought, saying, What shall we eat? or, What shall we drink? or, Wherewithal shall we be clothed? (for after all these things do the Gentiles seek:) for your heavenly Father knoweth that ye have need of all these things. But seek ye first the kingdom of God, and his righteousness, and all these things shall be added unto you. Take therefore no thought for the morrow: for the morrow shall take thought for the things of itself. Sufficient unto the day is the evil thereof." Matt. 6: 19—34.

This being the law, it is evident that law-abiding men cannot accumulate or keep vast estates. The possession of large wealth, carries with it a violent presumption of adultery against God. So Christ rules in the following saying:

'*Wo unto you that are rich! for ye have received your consolation.*' Luke 9: 24.

Three interesting cases, in which this rule is held to be sound law, are reported by the evangelists.

1. *The case of the rich young man.* "Behold, one came and said unto him, Good Master, what good thing shall I do, that I may have eternal life? And he said unto him, Why callest thou me good? there is none good but one, that is God: but if thou wilt enter into life, keep the commandments. He saith unto him, Which? Jesus said, Thou shalt do no murder, Thou shalt not commit adultery, Thou shalt not steal, Thou shalt not bear false witness; Honor thy father and thy mother; and, Thou shalt love thy neighbor as thyself. The young man saith unto him, All these things have I kept from my youth up: What lack I yet? Jesus said unto him, If thou wilt be perfect, go and sell that thou hast, and give to the poor, and thou shalt have treasure in heaven; and come and follow me. But

when the young man heard that saying, he went away sorrowful: for he had great possessions. Then said Jesus unto his disciples, Verily I say unto you, that a rich man shall hardly enter into the kingdom of heaven. And again I say unto you, it is easier for a camel to go through the eye of a needle than for a, rich man to enter . into the kingdom of God." Matt. 19: 16—24.

2. *The case of the rich fool.* "He said unto them, Take heed and beware of covetousness; for a man's life consisteth not in the abundance of the things which he possesseth. And he spake a parable un-to them, saying, The ground of a certain rich man brought forth plentiful-ly: and he thought within himself, saying, What shall I do, because I have no room where to bestow my fruits? And he said, This will I do: I will pull down my barns, and build greater; and there will I bestow all my fruits and my goods. And I will say to my soul. Soul, thou hast much goods laid up for many years; take thine ease, eat, drink, and be merry. But God said unto him, Thou fool! this night thy soul shall be required of thee: then whose shall those things be, which thou hast pro-vided? So is he that layeth up treasure for himself, and is not rich to-ward God." Luke 12: 15—21.

3. *The case of Dives and Lazarus.* "There was a certain rich man, which was clothed in purple and fine linen, and fared sumptu-ously every day: and there was a certain beggar named Lazarus, which was laid at his gate full of sores, and desiring to be fed with the crumbs which fell from the rich man's table: moreover, the dogs came and licked his sores. And it came to pass that the beggar died, and was carried by the angel's into Abraham's bosom: the rich man also died, and was bu-ried. And in hell he lifted up his eyes, being in torments, and seeth Abraham afar off, and Lazarus in his bosom: and he cried and said, Fa-ther Abraham, have mercy on me, and send Lazarus, that he may dip the tip of his finger in water, and cool my tongue; for I am tormented in this flame. But Abraham said, Son, remember that thou in thy lifetime re-ceivedst thy good things, and likewise Lazarus evil things; but now he is comforted, and thou art tormented." Luke 16: 19—25.

The only evidence of crime put forward in these cases, is the possession of riches. Yet it would not be safe to rely on them as establishing an absolute rule, that the possession of riches is incompatible with salvation; for when the disciples asked, in view of what was said in the case of the rich young man, 'Who then can be saved?' Christ answered, 'With men this is impossible, but with God all things are possible.' These cases only show that in Christ's view the possession of wealth is *prima facie* evidence, creating a violent *presumption* of selfishness and adultery.

To show Christ's view of the enormity of the crime of adulterous lust for money, as compared with other more unpopular offenses, one or two facts may be mentioned.

1. According to John's report, Christ commenced his public ministry with the miracle of turning water into wine for the use of a wedding party, (thus apparently sanctioning convivialities which many condemn;) but the next thing he did was one of the boldest acts of vehemence against sin that the world ever witnessed ; and THE SIN at which he struck, was the higher adultery—the sin, not of drunkards or whoremongers, but of market-men and money-changers. The following is the evangelist's account of the affair :

"The Jews' passover was at hand ; and Jesus went up to Jerusalem, and found in the temple those that sold oxen and sheep and doves, and the changers of money sitting : and when he had made a scourge of small cords, he drove them all out of the temple, and the sheep, and the oxen ; and poured out the changers' money, and overthrew the tables ; and said unto them that sold doves, Take these things hence ; make not my Father's house an house of merchandize." John 2: 13—16.

2. He repeated this singular act near the close of his ministry, as Mark reports thus:

"They come to Jerusalem ; and Jesus went into the temple, and began to cast out them that sold and bought in the temple, and overthrew the tables of the money-changers, and the seats of them that sold doves ; and would not suffer that any man should carry any vessel through the temple. And he taught, saying unto them, Is it not written, My house shall be called of all nations the house of prayer ? but ye have made it a den of thieves." 11: 15—17.

These are the only instances in which Christ's abhorrence of crime attained the climax of resort to physical force.

3. The 'supreme scoundrel,' in the drama of which Christ was the supreme hero, was Judas Iscariot, not a drunkard, or a whoremonger, but a money-monger. And it is worthy of notice that he was provoked to his final crime of selling his master, by the dispute about the alabaster box, which Christ

decided against his covetousness, and in favor of the loving woman who had been an adulteress. Luke 26: 6—16. He went immediately from that dispute and made a contract with the chief priests to sell his Lord for thirty pieces of silver —an appropriate termination of the war which Christ had all along waged against the love of money.

CONCLUSION.

It is evident that Christ's vehement indignation was directed, not against the lower adultery, but against the higher adultery. And as every body knows that the higher adultery is very respectable at the present day, in church and state, while all the virtuous indignation of public sentiment is reserved for the lower adultery,—it follows that either Christ's view of the relative enormity of crimes was inverted and false, or modern moralists, like their Jewish predecessors, " STRAIN AT A GNAT AND SWALLOW A CAMEL."

APPENDIX TO PART III.

[*Reader.*—We began our interview, Mr. Freechurch, in the free and easy way of questions and answers. But after a while, you put me into a course of hard reading, and you have kept me poring over grave discourses, till I had almost forgotten you. When are you going to tell me about the Costs and Conditions of Communism, as you promised?

Mr. Freechurch.—I did intend to give you a course of reading on these subjects, and I have plenty of material. But you have read about enough for the present; and besides, you must have got some idea, by this time, of the main items of the Costs of Bible Communism by learning what Bible Communism is. I will keep the material I have on hand for another book, and, if you please I will close this session by rehearsing a short conversation, which you will find quite appropriate here, as it illustrates the close relationship between MARRIAGE and SLAVERY, which is a prominent point in several of the articles that you have just been studying.]

COLLOQUY,

Between Judge North, Major South, and Mr. Freechurch.

—

SCENE,—*Newspaperdom.*—JUDGE NORTH *and* MAJOR SOUTH *disputing, and in danger of coming to blows.* MR. FREECHURCH *interposes.*

Mr. Freechurch.—Gentlemen, be calm: there is a more rational way of getting satisfaction than this. Let us have a fair discussion. We will hear your attack and defense, and help you to a more judicious conclusion than running each other through with the sword.

Judge North.—Very well: I am willing to debate the subject with Major South.

Major South.—Commence then, Judge North, as you are the assailant.

Judge N.—I am always ready in so good a cause. I affirm, then, that slavery is an arbitrary institution, created by law, and contrary to natural liberty. All men are *created* free and equal.

Major S.—I affirm on the contrary, that the relation of master and servant is natural. Servitude, or the labor of one for another, exists everywhere: and slavery is only one form of this necessity.

Judge N.—It is a most cruel and oppressive form, you must admit, one under which horrible wrong and outrage is committed. Look at the frequent accounts of slaves being *whipped to death.*

Major S.—There are instances of cruel treatment, it is true, but they are exceptions, not chargeable to the system, which is naturally one of protection and confidence.

Judge N.—It is a *vicious system* in itself, because it gives unlimited *power*, and such power in the present state of human nature is sure to be oppressive. Ownership of man by man is wrong, and prolific of wrong.

Major S.—But the *law* protects slaves from abusive masters.

Judge N.—What is the law worth when its enactment and administration are entirely in the hands of the masters? Legal protection to the blacks, you know full well, is for the most part merely nominal, and applies only in extreme cases.

Major S.—At any rate, the slaves are happy; they do not ask your pity. You could not persuade them to leave their masters, or exchange their condition with your own free laborers.

Judge N.—This is no argument in favor of slavery; it only shows the degraded state of the slave. The noble instinct which chooses *liberty or death*, is all crushed out of him. His spirit is broken under the yoke. Then, he is treated as a brute in respect to his affections. Family ties are sundered without remorse, and the tenderest connections rudely broken. What can you say in defense of this cruelty?

Major S.—I affirm that slavery is sanctioned by the Bible. Moses and Paul both recognized it, and gave regulations concerning it.

Judge N.—The Bible *permitted* slavery on account of the barbarism of the times, but certainly did not sanction it with any thing like approval; on the contrary, its whole spirit is opposed to it, and fully carried out, would lead to its immediate abolition. Furthermore, slavery is a system that recognizes no Bible. So far as the slave is concerned, that book might as well never have been given. You take away his right to read and inquire the way of life for himself; and if he ever gains a knowledge of religious duty, your monstrous claim of ownership is still paramount. He has no liberty to follow the dictates of his own conscience. Thus, by your power to heathenize and coerce him, all spiritual as well as bodily freedom is taken away.

Major S.—Did you ever think of the *consequences* which your fanaticism would lead to? The liberation of the slaves would be attended with pillage and bloodshed. Your tender mercy to them is murder to their masters.

Judge N.—I contend that *liberty breeds virtue*, and that the slaves, if liberated and treated justly, would be better citizens than they are now.

Major S.—Another consequence of your abolition notions would be to destroy the negroes themselves. They are not fit for liberty—not capable of taking care of themselves. Their masters would have to support them or they would starve.

Judge N.—This is a false assumption: for it is universally proved that free labor is more profitable than slave labor. The slaves would do their work more cheerfully and better, for wages, than they do from the fear of the lash.

Major S.—Just compare our servants with the free negroes of the North, and say which class is the happiest? You cannot deny that the lot of the slave is vastly preferable.

Judge N.—If this were so, it is because our free negroes suffer the disgrace and abasement of their brethren: so that their wretchedness is still owing to the existence of slavery. Slavery is a curse to the whole African race.

Major S.—Well, be that as it may, it is the corner-stone of our republican edifice. Your abolition principles strike at the very foundations of society. Besides, it is intermeddling with what does not concern you. The South have a right to their own domestic institutions, and this Northern interference is intolerable; for one, I am ready to defend my rights at the point of the sword.

Judge N.—'Justice must be done if the heavens fall.' A state of society founded on unrighteous principles ought to be subverted; and I shall not cease agitation against slavery, if it stirs up war.

Mr. Freechurch.—Before you proceed to such extremities, allow me a few words with Judge North. Perhaps I shall be able to divert your mutual wrath. Will you be moderator, Major South?

Major S.—Of course, with pleasure—proceed.

Mr. F.—Judge North, I hold the same opinion about marriage that you do of slavery, that it is an arbitrary institution, and contrary to natural liberty. What do you say to this opinion?

Judge N.—I say that it is manifestly false—nature every where dictates marriage.

Mr. F.—It dictates sexual union, I will allow; but this marriage in pairs is only one form or method of bringing about sexual union, and I believe that this method is as arbitrary as the slaveholder's method of securing natural service; and it is very extensively if not universally, a cruel and oppressive method of uniting the sexes, especially to woman, the weaker party. The catalogue of woman's abuses, under the tyranny of matrimony, compares very well with the cruel lot of the slaves. Let me read, for instance, an account of a conjugal mauling and murder, which I cut from a late paper:—

"OUTRAGE AND PROBABLE MURDER.—An examination has been going on at Albion, during the past week, of Mr. Lowder, residing in the town of Yates, about fifteen miles north of that village, for the supposed murder of his wife. The facts brought to light on the testimony of the neighbors and daughter of the prisoner, show a degree of depravity—of relentless, fiend-like cruelty, which it is seldom our lot to record. It appeared in evidence that he had been in the habit, for several weeks previous to her death, of treating his wife with the most wanton cruelty as a pastime—had knocked her down on several occasions with an ax-helve; would place

her repeatedly on the bed, jerk it from the bed-stead to the floor, and after beating her without mercy, would replace the bed and repeat the act. On one occasion it was said that after repeating the transaction described above several times, he raised the cellar-door, threw her into the cellar and kept her there till morning. The circumstances of her death were that she went to bed in usual health, and was found dead in the morning. When the coroner's inquest was held, Dr. Huff of Albion took the stomach to his residence, in which was detected, on examination, a considerable quantity of oxalic acid. It appeared that Mr. Lowder had purchased poison a short time previous to this event, and that a paper of white powder, admitted to be poison by him, had been found in the bed by his daughter."
—*Lockport (N. Y.) Courier.*

Judge N.—This is an extreme case. You will find such abuses only among the lowest classes, and they cannot be charged to the marriage system.

Major S.—But I said the same, you will recollect, of bad treatment of the slaves.

Mr. F.—The truth is, marriage gives man *the power of ownership* over woman; and such power is as wrong and prolific of wrong in the case of marriage, as in that of slavery.

Major S.—You must see the force of this argument, I am sure, Judge North.

Judge N.—But the *law* protects a woman from the violence of her husband. No man can commit a serious outrage against his wife without being punished.

Mr. F.—The law is nominally a defense, I admit; but recollect who has the control and administration of the law, and the natural reluctance and in some cases perhaps the danger, that would keep women from appearing as complainants against their husbands, and you will readily see that legal protection is available to married women only in extreme cases, and as a last resort.

Judge N.—Woman is nevertheless devotedly attached to marriage. You will make yourself perfectly odious to her, by advocating its abolition.

Mr. F.—The fact that the victims of marriage are attached to it, and could not be induced to abandon their situation, may be only a proof of their degradation. The Hindoo woman chooses to be burned with the body of her husband, because she knows no other way, and prefers death to the odium of unfashionable behavior.

Maj. S.—You will recollect, Judge, your inference against slavery on similar grounds.

Judge N.—Well, it is nonsense to think of comparing the marriage-system of civilization with an institution like slavery, that separates families and tramples on all the ties of blood.

Mr. F.—This is precisely the charge I was about to make against marriage. What can be more obvious than that marriage is the great separator of brothers and sisters and parents and children? In every instance union at the *altar*, as it is justly called, (considering the cruelty of the sacrifice,) mutilates two family circles. Weddings are frequently as woeful to the parent families as funerals. Examples of the rending of family ties are at hand. My father's family saw one of its daughter's exiled to the south, and another to the west, and both hurried to their graves by uncongenial climates and hardships. My friend here, Mr. M., has brought up a large family of children, and yet now in his old age he and his wife have been obliged to go 50 or 60 miles to meet an 'Orphan's Friend Society' for the purpose of getting a child of strangers to live with them. Marriage has taken all their children away.

Judge N.—But the Bible sanctions marriage, and you must admit it is a divine institution. 'Thou shalt not commit adultery,' is one of the ten commandments.

Mr. F.—The Bible sanctions marriage only as it sanctions slavery—i. e. temporarily, and because the world, by reason of sin, has not hitherto been prepared for better institutions; but it expressly declares in Matt. 22: 30, that in the final state of mankind marriage will be abolished; and that state all look for, and at least pray for as often as they use the Lord's prayer—'thy kingdom come, thy will be done on earth as it is done in heaven.' If the decalogue sanctions marriage by the commandment, 'Thou shalt not commit adultery,' it also sanctions slavery by the commandment, 'Thou shalt not covet thy neighbor's man servant, nor his maid servant, nor his ox, nor his ass.' In the New Testament, the same discourse which enjoins love and obedience on husbands and wives, also enjoins forbearance on masters, and faithfulness and submission on slaves. You refer to the Bible for your defense of marriage; but have you never observed that the actual operation of this institution, like that of slavery, in multitudes of instances, is such as to subvert the Bible, and nullify its requirements? What is it but a huge Bastile of spiritual tyranny, giving to men and women the power to debar each other from the rights of conscience and the free enjoyment of their religious faith? Whoever has had an opportunity to observe, knows that under this institution jealousy works toward God as well as toward man, and that in many cases the awakening of affection toward God in a man or woman is a cause of alarm, and is systematically vetoed by the married partner. In fact a state of true gospel devotion to God, in a husband or wife, would be felt generally, as a serious infringement on the institution. Under the marriage contract parties can arrogate the claim of entire devotion and the right to exclude each other from the service of God. I need not argue this point; those who have ever attempted to leave the beaten track of the world's ways for the higher service of God, know what a power of martyrdom is concealed under the sacred mantle of marriage. It is hardly fair to hold the Bible responsible for more than a temporary sanction of such institutions as marriage and slavery, which in spirit tend to contravene the Bible.

Judge N.—But the abolition of marriage would lead to unbridled licentiousness and social ruin.

Mr. F.—I reply in your own words, that 'liberty breeds virtue;' and I maintain that free-love, or complex-marriage, combined with community of property, would annihilate the very sources of adultery, whoredom, and all sexual abuse. It is the poverty and compulsory abstinence of the marriage system, that genders these crimes in society. The sense of plenty would directly stimulate to chastity and self-control.

Major S.—Good. *Liberty breeds virtue,* Judge.

Judge N.—What would become of women and children, if it were not for the system of maintenance and care that marriage provides? They cannot take care of themselves, and they would fare hard if there were no responsible husbands.

Mr F.—They would certainly fare better under a system of free-labor and free-love in Association, than they do under the marriage system, where each family is at the mercy of one man. A responsible Association of men, is the protection secured to every woman and child, in the system I advocate.

Judge N.—Look at the forlorn condition of old maids and old bachelors, and especially the class of abandoned women. What a contrast with the happy family relations of married life.

Mr. F.—These outsiders, my friend, are the 'free negroes' of the marriage system—that is, their position and degradation result from the existence of marriage, just as the degradation of the free blacks results from the existence of slavery. You can see for yourself that the abolition of marriage would have the same effect upon their condition that the abolition of slavery would have upon the negroes of the North. Their reproach would be taken away, and the genial influence of equality and restored self-respect would give them new motives of improvement.

Major S.—You have furnished your opponent with every argument so far, Judge.

Judge N.—But this is interfering with private rights, which no man of spirit will consent to. It strikes at the foundations of the social structure.

Major S.—'Justice must be done if the heavens fall,' Judge North.— Remember the story of the Farmer and the Lawyer, in the old spelling book, and abide by your own decision in our dispute.

Judge N.—I see I am in a snare. These ideas certainly must be taken into consideration. I must either let slavery alone, or go for a revolution of society at the North as well as at the South.

Mr. F.—I advise both parties to go for the kingdom of God, in which neither slavery or marriage covers wrong, but love works righteousness in freedom. [Exeunt Omnes.